4/02

25.^{00}

D0046266

Margaret O. Hyde and
John F. Setaro, M.D.

When the **BRAIN** Dies First

Franklin Watts
A Division of Grolier Publishing
New York London Hong Kong Sydney
Danbury, Connecticut

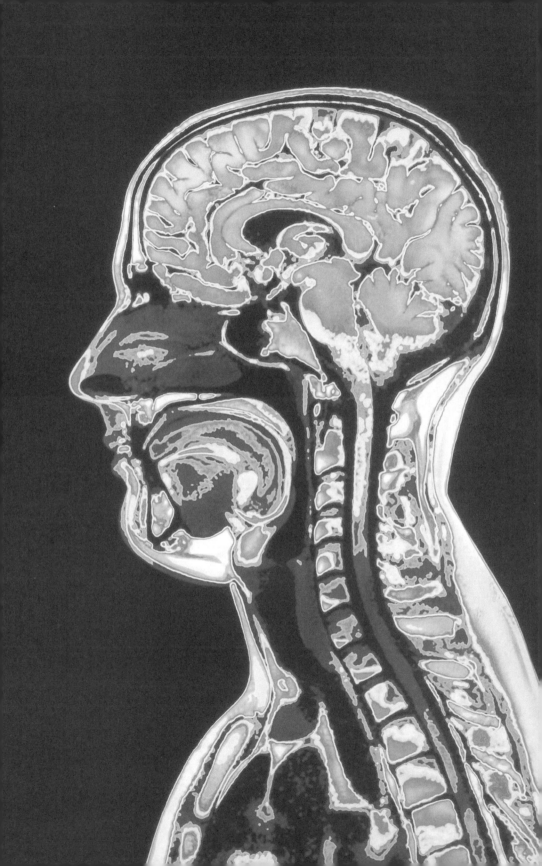

616.8
HYD
2000

When the BRAIN Dies First

Frontis: An MRI scan of the human head and shoulders
Photographs ©: Alzheimer's Association: 101, 103; AP/Wide World Photos: 55 (Michael Caulfield), 38 (John Redman), 12 (H. Rumph, Jr.), 84; Corbis-Bettmann: 58 (Frank Driggs), 51 (Reuters), 61, 93 (UPI), 87 (Jennie Woodcoock/Reflections Photolibrary), 42 (Tim Wright), 28; Custom Medical Stock Photo: 40 (Department of Clinical Radiology, Salisbury District Hospital/SPL), 76 (SPL); Index Stock Photography: 67, 74; Liaison Agency, Inc.: cover (Ferry), 36 (Christian Vioujard); Medichrome/StockShop: 20 (Brian Blauser), 70 (Howard Sochurok), 7 (David York); Medtronic: 65; National Institutes of Health: 14, 47; Peter Arnold Inc.: 108 (H. R. Bramaz), 29 (William Campbell), 11 (Alex Grey), 89 (Robert Holmgren); Photo Researchers: 69 (John Bavosi/SPL), 26 (Department of Clinical Radiology, Salisbury District Hospital/SPL), 34 (Ralph C. Eagle, Jr., MD.), 17 (Will & Deni McIntyre), 80 (SIU); PhotoEdit: 25 (Spencer Grant), 49 (Nourok); The Dana Alliance for Brain Initiatives: 110; Tony Stone Images: 79 (Bruce Ayres), 2 (David Job), 115 (Michael Rosenfeld), 23 (Karen Schulenburg).

Cover and interior design by Joan M. Toro

Visit Franklin Watts on the Internet at:
http://publishing.grolier.com

Library of Congress Cataloging-in-Publication Data

Hyde, Margaret O. (Margaret Olroyd).
   When the brain dies first / by Margaret O. Hyde and John F. Setaro.
      p.   cm.
   Includes bibliographical references and index.
   Summary: Examines the functioning of the human brain, various causes that impede its proper functioning, and research into prevention and treatment of brain injuries and disorders.
   ISBN 0-531-11543-7
   1. Brain damage Juvenile literature. 2. Dementia Juvenile literature.   [1. Brain. 2. Brain—Wounds and injuries. 3. Brain—Diseases.]   I. Setaro, John F. II. Title.
RC387.5.H94   2000
616.8—dc21   99-33060
                                                                  CIP

© 2000 by Franklin Watts
All rights reserved. Published simultaneously in Canada.
Printed in the United States of America.
2 3 4 5 6 7 8 9 10 R 09 08 07 06 05 04 03 02 01

CONTENTS

Brains Alive Beneath the Skull

Jason's brain was alive when he and his friends were walking home from school. Suddenly some kids from a neighborhood gang jumped from behind a fence and hit him on the head with a length of pipe. His friends called 911 and the ambulance arrived in minutes. Jason was rushed to the hospital emergency room where a team of doctors sprang into action. They monitored his vital functions—checking oxygen supply, blood pressure, control of seizures—and dealt with the problems of infection, the swelling of tissues, and bleeding. They inserted a drain to remove some of the fluid that was building up around his injured brain. But nothing could be done to repair the nerve cells that had been crushed and had died when the pipe penetrated his skull. Doctors could repair the damage to his body but not to his brain.

Jason lived on for a year. He never spoke another word nor showed any sign of hearing anything said to him. Parts of his brain were dead.

A brain can die in many different ways before the body dies. Head injury is so common that it has been called the silent epidemic. It is the number-one killer and cause of disability among young people in the United States.[1] Diseases, toxins, and drugs are other killers of brain tissue. Some rare brain viruses can act so quickly that a person can go to bed feeling only slightly ill and never wake up. With other diseases of the brain, it may take twenty years or more before their effects are seen.

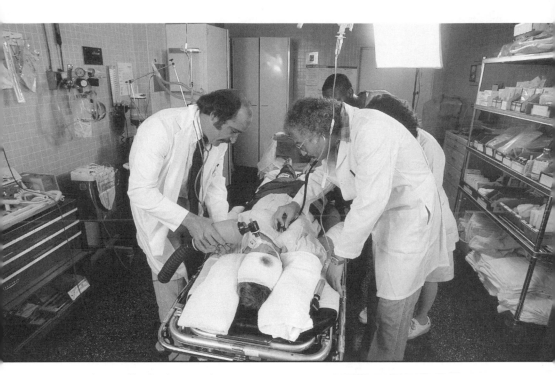

The staff of a hospital emergency room treats an accident victim with a head injury.

At some point in your life, you will be affected by a disease or disorder of the brain, either directly or through the experience of a friend or family member.[2] The number of people who suffer from a variety of head injuries and many kinds of dementia (loss of intellectual functioning) is increasing.

By the year 2050, the young people of today will live in a world with nearly 9 million people over the age of 85.[3] As the population of the United States ages, degenerative diseases such as Alzheimer's disease will become nearly four times as prevalent.[4] This disease progresses over two to twenty years and affects all family members. Financing the care of millions of people whose brains die before their bodies will increase the strain on the already overburdened health care system.

Understanding more about how and why brain cells die and investigating possible ways to prevent and cure diseases, as well as to care for those who suffer from them, are important for people of all ages.

Many Diseases Lead to Dementia

Often when the brain dies, or is severely injured, and the body remains alive, the person suffers from dementia. Originally dementia meant madness or insanity. Today most people associate dementia with Alzheimer's disease, but dementia actually means the loss of mental powers from any cause.

Dementia is the fourth most common cause of death in the United States.[5] Whether or not it is treatable depends on the kind of disease that causes it, but these disorders often lead to death. Few people had heard of kuru before the recent publicity about mad cow disease. Some forms of dementia are well known; others are uncommon. But when the brain dies first—before the body—the process of dying may be especially long, difficult, and painful.

The Healthy Brain

The healthy brain is very much alive. If you could see your brain, you would think that it looks quiet and more or less the same over large areas. But under the surface, your delicate brain is highly energetic. Electrical and chemical signals are traveling at unbelievable speeds among so many cells that your mind cannot begin to imagine what is going on inside your head. Inside your skull lies the most complex structure in the known universe.

Your brain—a wrinkled 3.5-pound (1.6-kg) mass of watery tissue that would fit inside a quart container—orchestrates behavior, movement, feeling, and sensation. Your heart beats at the brain's command; your lungs are directed to breathe. Fast-flowing messages direct the functioning of all your vital organs without your thinking about them. Important functions that are controlled by specialized areas in your brain work together to enable you to see stars mil-

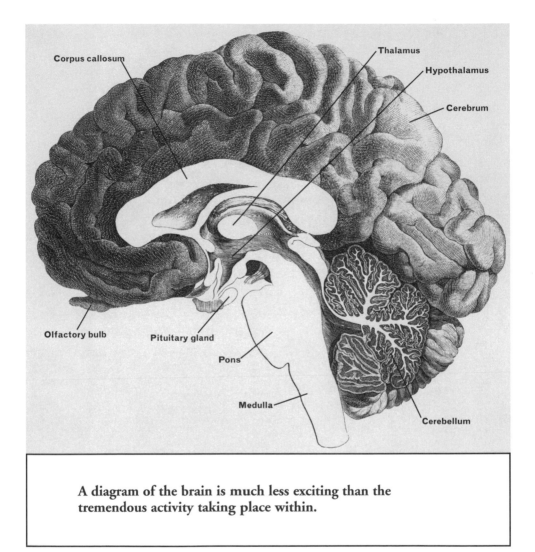

A diagram of the brain is much less exciting than the tremendous activity taking place within.

lions of miles away, to surf the Internet, and to behave in an infinite variety of ways.

The brain at work is called the mind. The mind constitutes the brain's programs, its total set of manipulations of symbols. The brain is the hardware; passion and reflection, thought and emotion, are aspects of the mind. The mind is what the brain does.

Looking at the Brain

If the top of your thick, bony skull were removed—as the top of the shell may be removed from a hardboiled egg—the view would not be very exciting. Folded and convoluted with wrinkles and ridges, the spongy material of a living brain is pinkish-gray in color: in a dead brain it is grayer. The surface rind, or cerebrum, is 2 mm thick (about an eigth of an inch) and overlies the visible part.[6] The folds of the cerebral cortex, the gray matter on the surface of the brain, make it possible for nearly two and a half feet of it (about 76 cm) to fit inside the skull.[7] Stretched flat this surface would be approximately the size of an office desk. You could see less than half of this surface area if you looked down at the outside of the whole brain.

The brain has been described as looking like a large hunk of shapeless creamy-pinkish fat,[8] about the consistency of tapioca pudding. If the skull did not contain it, the brain would collapse like a glob of jelly.[9] The two halves, or hemispheres, of the brain are connected by a narrow bridge of nerve fibers through which they communicate.

The hemispheres look alike but they function quite differently. In most people, the left brain is concerned with language, writing, reading, and other "reasoning abilities." The right brain is more concerned with spatial relationships, arithmetic, and artistic abilities. However, many aspects of these and other functions are spread through the brain.[10]

Brain Signals

Inside the apparently quiet living brain, signals travel through immense numbers of pathways, sometimes at speeds of almost 250 miles per hour (402 kph).[11] The nerve cells, or neurons, look a bit like microscopic trees. Each of the brain's billions of neurons is connected directly or indirectly to every other neuron. Other kinds of brain cells, known as glial cells, support and nourish the neurons. A neuron can receive a huge number of messages from many other neurons, and it may send an immense number of messages as well.[12] Some messages combine with others from a variety of sources; some

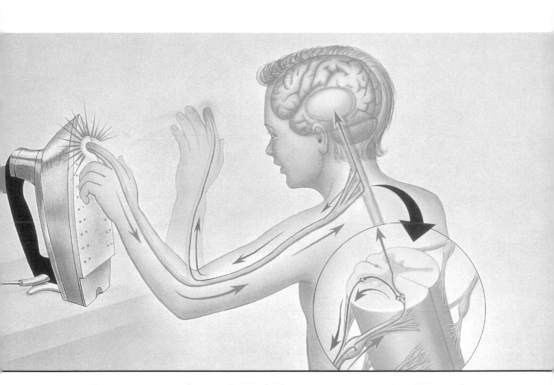

The perception of pain through the sensory nervous system, and a response from the motor nervous system

begin together at one distant source, then separate and go to many areas. Some signals loop back and forth traveling over the same path again and again.[13]

Neurons exist in many shapes. An unbelievable number of them send messages over immense numbers of pathways to regulate the body's functions and behavior. Years ago, your grandparents were probably taught the following about the brain: "You touch a hot iron, a message travels through a neuron to your brain. In your brain, a message travels through another nerve cell that is connected with a third neuron in your arm. This cell carries the message down your arm to your finger and the finger jumps away from the iron." Speed was considered the most miraculous part of this action. You moved a finger without even thinking about it. Today, we know that what happens is far more complicated. Millions of neurons may be activated. All this happens in a tiny fraction of a second.[14]

Brains and Computers

Computer experts who have worked many years with artificial intelligence (a branch of computer science that tries to mimic human intelligence) are awed by the human brain's complexity. These experts are trying to learn more about how the brain works in order to imitate it. Early in 1997, a chess-playing computer known as Deep Blue defeated a human world chess champion, Gary Kasparov. For decades, the chess world had been debating the possible outcome of a match between a computer and a grandmaster of chess. Deep Blue could analyze two hundred possible moves every second. This is a hundred times the calculating

Gary Kasparov, reigning world chess champion, matches his skill against Deep Blue, the computer chess champion.

ability of humans. It is more difficult to program a computer to remember the plot of "Little Red Riding Hood" than to remember a twenty-digit number, but a person who can easily retain the story may find it impossible to remember the number.[15]

Today's computers can perform numerous difficult feats, such as controlling mechanical arms, recognizing human speech, prescribing correct medications, and predicting epidemics. But according to Steven Pinker, director of the Center for Cognitive Science at M.I.T. (Massachusetts Institute of Technology), four-year-old humans have a far greater ability to see, talk, or use common sense than these machines.[16]

Although the brain's processors are slower and less exact than those in supercomputers, there are hundreds of billions of them, each connected to thousands of others that can recognize complicated patterns in an instant. In this and many other ways, the human brain surpasses the computer. The information-processing capacity of the most powerful supercomputer has been equated with that of a snail's brain.[17]

Connections

The number of neurons in your brain—about 100 billion—has been compared to the number of stars in the Milky Way. But the number of nerve cells is not as important as the number of complex connections among these cells. Each of the billions of nerve cells may have more than a thousand points of contact at synapses—the minute spaces between nerve cells. The 100 billion neurons of the brain have 60 trillion synapses.[18]

Most of the activity of the brain involves communication between cells and fibers by means of electrical impulses set off by chemical messengers that are called neurotransmitters. At least fifty kinds of neurotransmitters have been discovered, and many of them may be involved in bridging the gaps at synapses.

Most neurons have three parts: the cell body, composed of a nucleus coated by a sticky fluid; a long stem known as an axon; and many shorter stems known as dendrites. The cell bodies make up the brain's gray matter; white sheaths on axons and dendrites form the white matter.[19]

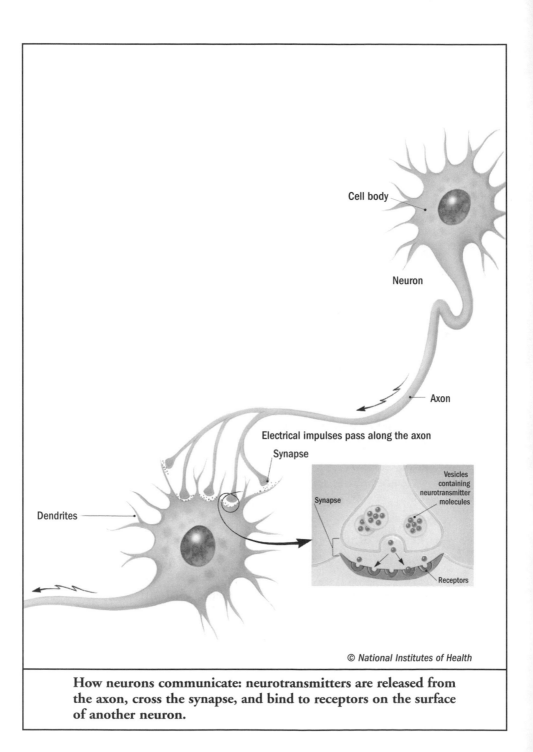

How neurons communicate: neurotransmitters are released from the axon, cross the synapse, and bind to receptors on the surface of another neuron.

Messages travel along dendrites to the cell body and the axons. The dendrites are often described as information receivers. Neurotransmitters ferry signals across synapses and lock on to the receptors of the dendrites of the next neuron. The total number of connections within this network is unimaginable.

The Complex Brain

The scientific era of brain research that began in the nineteenth century has progressed at an increasingly rapid rate. More has been learned about the organization and function of the human brain during the past twenty years than in the previous two hundred years.[20] In spite of this, scientists are just dipping their toes into the vast ocean of information about the brain that remains to be explored.

Decades of study have revealed the specific functions of various regions of the brain, and scientists have named the bulges and grooves on its surface. Volumes of published research describe how the parts of the brain work together and what happens when some minute part does not work, but a tremendous amount of research lies ahead. The quest to understand the workings of the brain has been called the last frontier of science.

CHAPTER TWO

Shaken Baby Syndrome and Other Closed Head Injuries

From before birth until death, the brain can suffer a wide variety of injuries. In the United States, about 2 million head injuries occur each year, and 500,000 of the injured are hospitalized. Two-thirds of all head-injured patients are younger than thirty.[1] Many of the injuries are closed head injuries, in which there is no opening in the skull.

Cerebral Palsy

Cerebral palsy, a disease in which there is muscular weakness, can result when a baby's brain is damaged due to an accident, an illness such as meningitis, lead poisoning, or repeated beating or shaking. It may also be caused by something that affects the brain before birth, such as incompatibility between the baby's and mother's blood, alcohol use, or German measles during pregnancy; premature birth or lack of oxygen to the central nervous system during birth; or a metabolic disorder. Many problems involving movement are caused by damage to the brain.

In most cases of cerebral palsy, damage to the brain is not serious enough to cause death, but there is a wide range of impairment. Josh is a ten-year-old whose cerebral palsy makes it difficult for him to accomplish even simple movements, such as reaching for a cup. His arm jerks so much that he often has to make several attempts to grasp it.

In some people with cerebral palsy there is a stiffness or floppiness in their movements in general, or there may be a

A wide variety of physical therapy programs—including riding lessons—are used with cerebral palsy patients.

twisted posture. Cerebral palsy is the most common crippling disorder of childhood.[2]

Shaken Baby Syndrome

The act of shaking a baby has been implicated in many cases of brain-damaged infants.[3] Kevin was only two months old when he was rushed to the hospital in the middle of the night. His convulsions—involuntary and violent movements of his body—were frightening. Doctors in the emergency room began treating his symptoms while a nurse asked his mother and father questions about what had happened at home in the past few hours. Did someone shake Kevin? Did he hit his head on the crib or the wall when he was shaken? The nurse questioned Brian, Kevin's father, especially closely. He kept repeating, "I didn't mean to hurt him."

Brian explained that he loved the baby, but the crying night after night made him tired and angry. This night, he became so upset that he lifted Kevin out of his crib and shook him hard to try to stop the crying. He thought Kevin might have hit his head on the crib, but there was no bleeding. His head looked fine. Could the shaking have something to do with the convulsions?

When Kevin's convulsions stopped, a doctor told his parents that there had been some bleeding and swelling inside the baby's skull. There is little space for swelling inside the brain's bony case. Swelling reactions are the most common cause of serious brain injuries.[4]

Kevin's doctor, who was a specialist in child abuse, told Brian that many people are not aware of how dangerous it is to shake a baby, but head trauma is now known to be the most frequent cause of permanent disability or death among abused infants and children.[5] The doctor made it clear that, though he understood how Brian felt, what he had done was wrong, and he turned the case over to a social worker who dealt with child abuse. If Kevin died, Brian could be charged with murder.

In most cases of shaken baby syndrome, the parent or caregiver is reacting to inconsolable crying, but problems with toilet training or feeding, and interruption of television viewing, sometimes cause people to lose control and strike out.

Many parents, baby-sitters, and other caregivers who have shaken a baby in an effort to stop continued crying say that they were so upset they felt like shaking the life out of the baby. Some are horrified to find that they have. In 1997, a young British woman working in the United States, Louise Woodward, was accused of the death of a baby in her care after the eight-month-old was taken to the hospital with swelling of the brain and bleeding in the head and interior linings of the eye.[6] The baby died, perhaps because of shaking, but there was some question about former child abuse. Louise Woodward was found guilty of murder, but her sentence was reduced to involuntary manslaughter and she was released shortly after the trial.

Many doctors consider shaken baby syndrome to be a specific medical problem. Babies have large heads that are heavy for their bodies, their neck muscles are undeveloped, and their brain tissue is exceptionally fragile. The whiplash action created by shaking can cause the brain to bounce around in the skull. Vigorous shaking repeatedly pitches the brain in different directions. Blood vessels that connect the brain to the skull may tear, causing blood to pool inside the skull.[7]

Most experts agree that tossing a baby in the air, or bouncing one on a knee, will not inflict the type of injuries associated with shaken baby syndrome, although there is a slight chance that they will. Babies who have been tossed in the air have also been dropped, sometimes hitting their heads on concrete floors, coffee tables, and other objects.[8]

Recent studies, however, have questioned whether shaking alone is enough to cause bleeding in the brain. Many times the baby's head hits a hard surface, such as a crib rail or a wall, and the brain, which has been bouncing back and forth in a watery sea of protective fluid, stops suddenly. This rapid deceleration causes the brain to slam into the skull and blood vessels may rip loose. Blood oozes from torn vessels and forms clots, while fluid collects in the bruised areas of the brain. The swelling brain may choke off its own blood supply and cause fatal compression of the parts of the brain that control heartbeat and respiration.[9]

Victims of shaken baby syndrome, or shaken impact syndrome, can suffer from problems such as swelling of the brain, seizures, hearing loss, mental retardation, blindness, learning disabilities, or cerebral palsy; they may even die. The first twenty-four hours after an injury are critical, but many serious effects can appear later. The total extent of an injury may not be known for several days, or even longer.

About a thousand babies are hospitalized each year because parents or caregivers become so frustrated or angry that they shake the babies, causing serious brain damage. Many more infants may be injured in this way, but they go untreated and there are no records of them.[10]

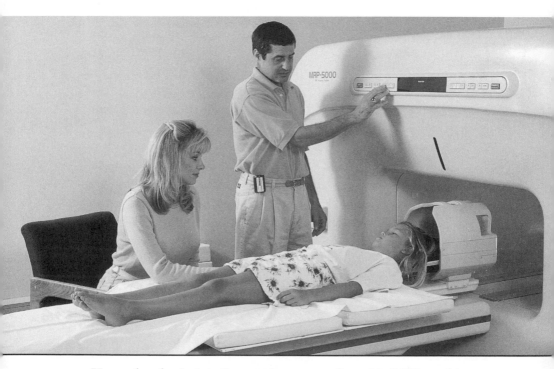

Up-to-date brain imaging equipment, such as this MRI machine, enables medical staff to make a rapid diagnosis of a brain injury.

The speed with which the diagnosis of a head injury is made can make the difference between a brain that lives and a brain that dies, no matter what the person's age. Hospitals with twenty-four-hour access to sophisticated brain-imaging equipment, and that have neurologists (specialists in nervous-system diseases and problems) available for immediate consultation provide the best chance of recovery for a person who has suffered a traumatic brain injury.

Blows to the Head

Many older children and adults suffer serious head injuries from blows received in fights, or bicycle, motorcycle, and automobile accidents; skiing, skateboarding, and other sports accidents; falls; and from other causes. Some boxers suffer permanent brain damage from a solid blow to the head. People who carry a gene identified as apoE4 are more vulnerable to "boxer's dementia" than those who do not.[11] It is clear that repeated trauma to the head can cause dementia.

The skull acts as a barrier that deflects most of the force of a blow to the head. Even when the skull is fractured, the brain may be left relatively unharmed because the skull has absorbed so much of the force. The cerebrospinal fluid that surrounds the brain acts somewhat like an airbag to cushion blows.[12]

Sixteen-year-old Marcie was driving some friends to a local store when the car in front of her stopped suddenly. She could not avoid crashing into it, and almost immediately the car following her ran into her rear bumper. Marcie was not wearing a seat belt, and her head hit the windshield hard. Upon impact, her head stopped moving forward, and her brain, which floats relatively free within the skull, maintained its motion because of inertia. Her moving brain collided with her skull, causing a concussion, an injury to the brain.

The blow to Marcie's head was so severe that she lost consciousness for a short time. A more severe impact may leave a person unconscious for a long time, in a condition known as a coma. The length of time during which a person loses consciousness is usually related to the seriousness of the brain damage. Even though Marcie regained consciousness quickly, her friends wisely insisted that she go to the hospital.

Marcie felt dizzy, had double vision, and had trouble remembering what had happened. She could not think clearly for the rest of the day. She needed a thorough examination to determine the extent of the damage from the blow to her head.

Blows to the head produce a variety of symptoms. A minor cut on the head may bleed a lot because there are many blood vessels on the scalp. A person who does not bleed or even lose consciousness may actually be seriously impaired, while another person may walk away from a major collision and suffer no significant injury.[13] Even if there seems to be no damage to a victim's brain, a severe blow to the head should be followed by a doctor's examination.

Loss of consciousness, vomiting, drowsiness, and seizures are all signs of damage to brain tissue. If an accident occurs late in the day, the injured person should be awakened periodically during the night to make certain that he or she can be woken and is not confused or disoriented.

A blow to the head may cause damage that cannot be traced to a specific part of the brain. This type of injury is called diffuse. If the blow is hard, it can cause bruising and permanent brain damage leading to future seizures. An observer cannot judge how the impact affects the brain. The jarring can tear, stretch, or twist microscopic blood vessels, fibers, and nerve cells, and their connections may never return to their former condition.[14]

Sports coaches are told to watch football players and other athletes for at least twenty minutes after a blow to the head to make certain they do not exhibit changes in behavior such as lack of alertness, loss of coordination, inability to concentrate, or slowed reactions.[15]

Bicycle accidents are responsible for many head injuries. About six hundred bicyclists under the age of fourteen die from accidents every year in the United States. Head injuries are the primary cause in about 80 percent of these fatalities. Helmets are the best hope of protecting the riders' brains from

Safety helmets protect bicyclists at all levels of skill from brain injuries.

the effects of bicycle and motorcycle accidents. Helmets are also recommended for skiing, in-line skating, and skateboarding. Seat-belt requirements, the use of helmets in a wide variety of sports, and education about what to do after a hard bump to the head, are helping to reduce the number of cases of permanent damage from head injuries.

Although most blows to the head do not cause serious damage because the skull and the cerebrospinal fluid cushion the brain, head injuries are one of the most widespread and devastating health hazards in America today.

CHAPTER THREE

Breaking and Entering the Skull

Without the protection of the skull, brain cells quickly die. The skull was not designed for easy opening, but unfortunately accidents may crack it apart. Sometimes neurosurgeons invade the skull of a patient, using specially designed drills and saws. These doctors' skills save the lives of people whose injured or diseased brains are dying, leaving other parts of their bodies disabled.

A Crack in the Skull

Courtney suffered a life-threatening injury, a crack in her skull, after a collision between her bike and a small truck. When she reached the emergency room, a small amount of pinkish-gray brain tissue was visibly oozing from the crack in her skull. She was awake but her speech was confused. Nurses quickly cut away her clothing and put her in military antishock trousers—inflatable pantaloons known as a MAST suit—designed to force blood to her brain. A doctor cleaned the wound on the right side of her head, first removing gauze that the paramedics had stuffed into the opening to contain the bleeding. The doctor also removed blood-caked hair and splinters of glass that had come from the truck windshield. An intern stitched the skin above the wound temporarily, knowing that a neurosurgeon would reopen it soon.

After X-rays showed that there was no major damage to Courtney's neck or back, the medical staff removed the cervical collar paramedics had placed on her at the scene of the accident and lifted her off the backboard they had placed her on

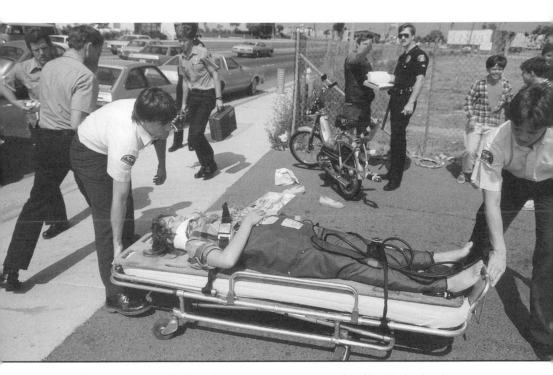

Emergency medical technicians use a cervical collar and a backboard to protect an accident victim from further injury.

before moving her to the ambulance. She was placed in a CT (computerized tomography) scanner that made a composite picture of X-rays of her brain. Then she was taken to an operating room where a neurosurgeon used sophisticated tools to try to limit the damage to her brain and to close her skull.

Courtney was fortunate to be treated at a large trauma center for a week after the accident, where doctors were able to carefully monitor the swelling that occurs after brain injury. Whether she would recover, or survive with effects that would mean a different kind of life, or even survive at all, remained a question.

Pressure in the Brain

In the past two decades, medical research has demonstrated that not all brain-cell death occurs at the moment of an acci-

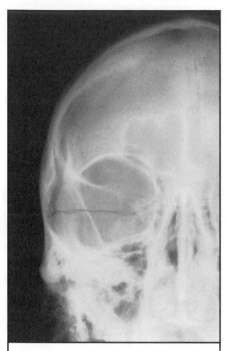

An X-ray image shows a fractured skull. The fracture can be seen as a long, dark, horizontal line at the left, center.

dent. Some damage may evolve over hours, or even days, and this damage may be preventable.[1] A number of doctors are leading a movement to alert medical personnel to the need for monitoring of pressure in the brain after head injury.

As soon as a seriously brain-injured person reaches a major hospital, emergency care begins. This may include use of a ventilator, X-rays, a CT scan, and other tests. In many hospitals, a small hole is drilled in the skull and a silicon tube (catheter) is inserted. This creates a drain for the excess cerebrospinal fluid in which the brain floats. Normally, the brain maintains a balance between the amount of cerebrospinal fluid that is produced and the amount that is absorbed. This fluid fills all the space inside the skull that is not filled by brain or blood.[2] When the brain is injured, the brain volume increases due to swelling, but the skull is inflexible, and there is no room for the brain to expand. In any trauma patient, the increased pressure in the skull makes it more difficult for the blood to circulate to the brain and supply it with the oxygen it needs. Without oxygen, brain cells quickly die

A Bullet in the Brain

Automobile accidents and shootings are two of the common causes of skulls being opened. Marvin's skull was invaded by a bullet that traveled all the way through his head, destroying the brain tissue along its path. He looked young and healthy as he lay on the hospital gurney—except for the small, oozing wound in his skull. The bullet and bone fragments in his brain appeared white in the X-rays on the light board. After a neurosurgeon studied the films, the staff doctor and two medical students rolled the gurney down the hall to the elevator that would take Marvin to the operating room. As they moved down the corridors, one of the students helped Marvin breathe by repeatedly squeezing air from a rubber bag through a tube and face mask and into his lungs.

When Marvin reached the imaging department, technicians slid him into the CT scanner that would provide the surgeon with a three-dimensional image of his brain. Now the surgeon could plan the operation to remove the embedded pieces of bullet and bone. On the operating table, the area around the entry wound was cleared of blood and a piece of shattered bone was removed. Special instruments were used to nip away at the edges of the hole in Marvin's skull, and the piece of bullet that was near the surface was removed. Another piece of bullet more deeply lodged in his brain would have to remain because its removal was too dangerous to attempt. It would be impossible to remove this piece of bullet without taking some brain with it, and neurosurgeons have great respect for brain tissue. Every bit of brain is very important, and they touch as little as possible.

Since there were no blood clots or bleeding in Marvin's brain, doctors sewed up the dura—the hard, fibrous membrane just below the skull that is rich with blood vessels and nerves.[3] They closed the entry wound, then they worked on the exit wound. Another bullet fragment was removed from this area, and the wound was closed after a catheter was inserted to allow excess fluid to drain.

Marvin's recovery would depend on which parts and how much of his brain had been damaged. His parents were warned that he might suffer weakness or paralysis, or have seizures or speech difficulties. A bullet entering the brain can cause a persistent coma or death due to loss of all brain function or to cardiac arrest. Even if a patient makes a full recovery, there can be changes in behavior, such as speech difficulties and memory problems.

Brain Tumors

Neurosurgery—the science and art of operating on the brain by opening the skull—has changed a great deal in recent years. Surgeons perform operations that range from the removal of small tumors to the removal of half a brain. Since the 1980s, many surgeons have had the help of stereotactic frames—aluminum frames that are bolted to the skull of the patient while he or she is under local anesthesia. Graphite pins are drilled into the skull so the position of the frame relative to the tumor cannot change, while a computerized scanner identifies the exact position of the tumor.[4] In the operating room, a metal arm guides a biopsy needle for tissue removal to the target designated by computer-guided coordinates.

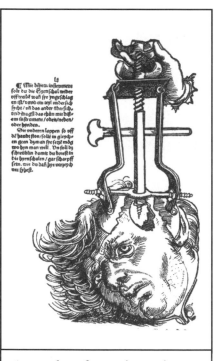

A woodcut from about the sixteenth century shows the techniques used in brain surgery in that period.

The development of new equipment enables surgeons to see things they could not have seen twenty-five years ago.[5] Two microscopes, for instance, allow two doctors to have the same view as they carefully work their way into the center of a human brain to find and remove a tumor.[6]

Some neurosurgeons are learning to save brain

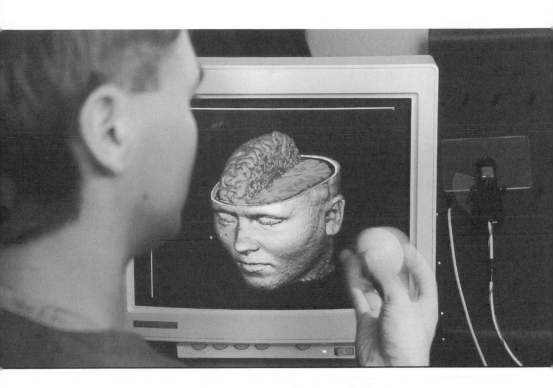

A neurosurgeon studies a 3-D visualization of a brain.

tissue by preplanning operations using three-dimensional holograms—photographs produced by reflected laser beams. Images of a patient's brain in exquisite detail can be mechanically rotated on a screen in the operating room to reduce the chances that the surgeon will disturb healthy tissue while removing a tumor.[7]

About 40,000 Americans are diagnosed with brain tumors each year.[8] A benign tumor does not contain cancer cells, but it can press on sensitive areas of the brain and cause trouble. Malignant brain tumors contain cancer cells that are likely to grow rapidly and crowd, or invade, the tissue around them. They may put out roots, somewhat like a plant's, that may burrow into healthy brain tissue and kill it, or they may be enclosed in a capsule.[9] In many cases, brain tumors are cancers that have spread to the brain from the lungs, breasts, or other parts of the body.

Sometimes tumors grow in one of the three layers that enclose the brain. These wrappings are called the meninges. If they are infected with bacteria, a person suffers from meningitis, a disease that can lead to brain death. Often tumors in the meninges are small and harmless, but some tumors in the meninges may press on the brain and cause damage and even death if they are not removed.

Pressure from a brain tumor or blood clot may lead to many serious conditions, including loss of understanding, speech, or voluntary movement, as areas controlling these functions are affected. If treatment is withheld, a brain may die before the body.[10]

Removing Sections of the Brain

Such great strides have been made in the field of brain surgery that even scientists are amazed at some of the excellent results.[11] One brain surgery technique developed in the last decade is called hemispherectomy, an operation in which half of the brain is removed. Dr. Ben Carson, a pediatric neurosurgeon at Johns Hopkins Pediatric Epilepsy Center, described the first time he removed half of a patient's brain.[12] His patient, Maranda, who was four years old in 1985, suffered from Rasmussen's syndrome, a rare disease that caused severe seizures at the rate of about a hundred a day. The inflammation and death of brain tissue progresses slowly and steadily in this viruslike illness, leading to permanent paralysis of one side of the body, mental retardation, and then death.

Maranda's mother sought help at many medical centers, but no one could offer treatment to stop the progressive deterioration of Maranda's brain. At Johns Hopkins she was told that there was something that might help, even though there were many risks involved: a radical operation in which half the brain is removed. The disease is confined to one side of the brain, although doctors do not know the reason for this, nor exactly what causes it.

After great consideration, Maranda's mother agreed to the procedure, fully aware that Maranda might die on the operating table. This possibility was weighed against the fact that her brain would continue to die without the operation. It was a last resort, but it was the only hope for the child. Even if she survived the surgery, there was a great risk that she would not be able to talk or that she would be paralyzed on one side. Earlier attempts at hemispherectomies had had poor results, with many patients dying during or after the operation. Others were left in a condition in which they would need constant care.[13]

To begin Maranda's operation, Dr. Carson drilled six small holes in her skull, connected them with an air-powered saw, and lifted away the left side of her skull to expose the outer covering of her brain. The operation took ten hours, with eight of the ten devoted to Dr. Carson inching away the inflamed left half of Maranda's brain. He had to coax away tissue without touching or injuring the fragile part that was still healthy. Maranda bled profusely, losing nine pints of blood during the operation, and doctors replaced twice that amount. When the skull had been carefully replaced with strong sutures, the surgical team relaxed, but they did not yet know what they had accomplished.

Only in young people is there enough plasticity in the brain so that the half that remains might take over functions of the half that has been removed. Maranda eventually talked and moved her arms and legs. Her seizures stopped after the operation. In subsequent years, she managed well without the left half of her brain.

Dr. John Freeman and his group of surgeons at Johns Hopkins Pediatric Epilepsy Center have performed hemispherectomies on more than fifty patients. Several dozen of these operations are performed each year in the United States.[14] Before surgery, some children have so many seizures that one blends into the next, despite heavy medication to try to control them. Scientists are not certain why the procedure stops seizures that cannot be controlled by medication.

Although deficits often result, such as weak hands and legs and some vision problems, having had half of their brain removed has improved the lives of young epileptics for whom no other treatment was helpful.

For the surgeons who enter the skull, the brain remains challenging and mysterious. Through many years of hard work, new instruments, advances in brain scans, and a heightened ability to stop bleeding, those who invade the brain are better able to help keep it alive.

CHAPTER FOUR

Brain Death by Infection

Any infection capable of attacking the brain is capable of destroying the mind. Most infectious brain diseases are caused by viruses, bacteria, fungi, or parasites, but in some cases the cause is unknown. In one group of diseases—spongiform disorders that cause microscopic holes in the brain—the nature of the disease agent is hotly debated. According to one theory, a newly discovered agent known as a prion may be responsible. Some critics of this theory believe that instead small viruses or another agent, small molecules known as virinos, may be responsible.[1] Virinos are camouflaged so the immune system does not pick them up.

Neurologist Stanley B. Pruisner of the University of California at San Francisco was awarded the Nobel prize in 1997 for discovering prions as a new biological principle of infection. According to his theory, prions are proteins found in every cell of the body. They are capable of propagating without the aid of DNA (deoxyribonucleic acid, the chemical compound in genes that carries the genetic code) or RNA (ribonucleic acid, the chemical that carries information from DNA and is involved in the formation of proteins). Sometimes the prions mutate and become abnormally shaped, and these mutants turn other normal prions into mutants. Mutant prions accumulate in the brain and cause diseases, such as kuru and Creutzfeldt-Jakob disease (CJD) in humans and bovine spongiform encephalitis in cows (mad cow disease), that lead to dementia.

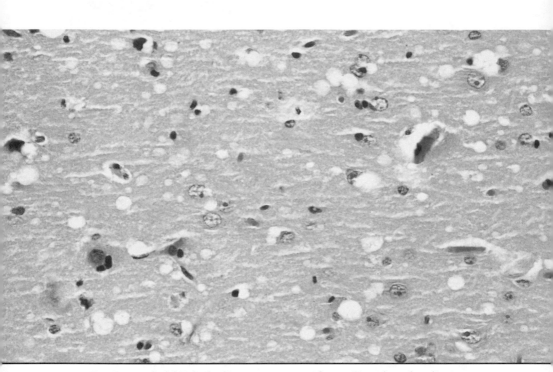

In Creutzfield-Jakob disease, a spongiform disorder, the disease agent causes microscopic holes in the brain, giving it a sponge-like appearance.

A number of respected researchers disagree with Dr. Pruisner's theory that spongiform diseases can be caused by mutant prions. They contend that the nature of the infectious agent is unknown.[2]

No matter what agent causes them, some scientists think that spongiform diseases may possibly be a threat to meat eaters around the world. The future course of mad cow disease and the possible relationship of prions to Alzheimer's and Parkinson's disease is one of the most intriguing and controversial mysteries in science today.

According to Richard Rhodes, author of *Deadly Feasts: Tracking the Secrets of a Terrifying New Plague,* the conditions exist in the United States for an epidemic of a native strain of bovine spongiform encephalitis.[3] If so, prevention of this untreatable, fatal disease that can be spread through the food supply is of major importance. But before you panic, consider the fact that Dr. Pruisner was quoted in the *San Francisco Chronicle* as saying that he ate an excellent steak on the day he heard about winning the Nobel prize. "I don't think we in America should be worried," he is quoted as saying.[4]

In the United States, brains and spinal cords of dead animals—the parts that might carry CJD—are not usually used in cattle food so they do not get into the food chain. But critics claim more needs to be done to protect Americans from eating infected material that may travel from cattle feed, to cattle, to products such as hamburger and bologna.[5] With public concern about the possibility of a mad cow disease epidemic in the United States, it is not surprising that diseases like kuru and CJD that affect a relatively small number of people are receiving much attention.

Doctors in Kentucky have warned people not to eat squirrel brains, a regional delicacy often served with scrambled eggs, because infected squirrels can carry the agent that causes CJD. Eleven cases of this southern version of mad cow disease have been diagnosed in Kentucky in the last four years, and all of them were in squirrel-brain eaters. If it were not for the concern about mad cow disease, these incidents would probably not be publicized.

Kuru

Kuru is a spongiform disease that was found among the Fore people of New Guinea, who are said to have lived as if they were in the Stone Age. Eating dead relatives was seen as a way of honoring them and it also provided a source of food. The Fore tribe is one of about seven hundred tribes that live in the mountainous rain forest regions of eastern New Guinea. Many tribe members suffered from kuru in the days when women and children who were kin and friends of a dead person ate the parts of the body that the men did not want at a funeral feast. Scientists who studied the tribe in the 1950s learned that some women and children who were at these

Examination of brain tissue can help researchers understand spongiform disease and other brain infections.

feasts developed kuru; but men, who did not eat the brains, were not affected.

Kuru was a fatal disease. Generations of Fore were familiar with the symptoms: an unsteady gait followed by tremors, then the loss of the ability to talk and swallow. In time, the victims of kuru became almost completely incapacitated and finally died.[6]

Vincent Zigas, an Australian public health officer stationed in the New Guinea eastern highlands, and Carleton Gajdusek, an American researcher who spent years among the Fore, described kuru in 1957. The disease was also known as the "laughing death," since it was accompanied by wide smiles and laughter for which there was no reason. Although sufferers remained alert and aware till near the end of their lives, autopsies revealed microscopic holes that made their brains look somewhat like a sponge.[7]

After the discovery of the relationship between cannibalism and kuru, the Fore practice of eating the dead was made illegal and the disease abated. The epidemic of kuru steadily tapered off, and no child has been afflicted in recent years.

Researchers noted that kuru and scrapie, a disease affecting sheep, appeared to have striking similarities. Both caused trembling and lack of coordination, and both produced a characteristic spongy appearance in the brain. Both diseases are fatal and infectious, meaning that they can be transmitted through the transplanting or ingesting of affected tissue.

Creutzfeldt-Jakob and Mad Cow Disease

Kuru and Creutzfeldt-Jakob disease (CJD) are diseases affecting humans that cause similar brain damage: holes in the brain. Infected individuals gradually become confused and disoriented. Their behavior becomes childlike and they can no longer reason. They stagger, twitch spasmodically, and lose their ability to control their bladders and to swallow. After death, the CJD is revealed through an autopsy of their brains.

CJD is uncommon, but not rare, appearing in about one person per million worldwide—a higher rate than that of rabies.[8] Drs. Creutzfeldt and Jakob first described the disease that bears their names in reports that appeared in 1920 and 1921. By the end of the 1950s, it seemed evident that eating contaminated tissue spread kuru. It was known that scrapie was spread through the eating of the afterbirth of infected sheep, or was picked up from the land where infected sheep grazed.[9] How was CJD spread?

The first known transmission of CJD from human to human occurred in 1971 when a surgeon transplanted a cornea from a man who was later found to have had CJD.[10] The disease has apparently been transmitted in a small number of other cases in the following ways: corneal transplants, brain operations, and injections of growth hormone produced by human pituitary glands before the synthetic growth hormone used today became available.[11] About 10 to 15 percent of CJD cases appear to be inherited. But what causes the other cases?

In the past, CJD disease was usually confined to people between the ages of fifty-five and eighty, but recently a variant of CJD appeared in younger people in Britain. According to prevailing theory, these victims contracted it by eating beef from cows suffering from bovine spongiform encephalopathy (BSE). This disease became known as mad cow disease because the sick animals exhibit nervous and aggressive behavior. By the end of 1987, BSE had spread through herds in England

In England, fear of the spread of mad cow disease led to the slaughter of thousands of cows.

and Wales. The feeding of the ground, cooked, and dried remains of dead cattle and sheep to cattle in Britain as a protein supplement was implicated.[12] In June 1988, Richard Lacey, a young physician, argued for the slaughter of all infected herds in Britain, since the new variation of CJD appeared to come from eating contaminated beef.[13]

Some scientific evidence supported the theory that people were dying from eating contaminated meat and set off a panic in 1996. This led to the slaughter of over 37,000 cows in Britain in that year alone.[14] The United States had banned the importation of beef from Britain for a number of years, and in 1996 the World Health Organization recommended a global ban on the feeding of sheep, goat, cattle, and other animals to livestock to prevent the spread of spongiform diseases.[15]

An estimated 77 million Americans eat beef every day.[16] Whether eating beef is a "deadly feast" may not be known for many years, since the incubation period (the time from infection until symptoms) of spongiform diseases is two to thirty-five years.[17] While some people are concerned about the risk of this form of disease, others think they are overreacting. By 1997, twenty people, most in Britain, had been officially diagnosed with the new strain of CJD.[18] No one knows what the future will bring, but research continues.

Abscesses in the Brain

The causes of abscesses in the brain are well known. An abscess is much like a boil on the skin, where infected material composed of white cells and bacteria (pus) collects. In the case of AIDS patients, a common cause of brain abscesses is a parasite known as toxoplasma. Bacteria can enter the brain through the bloodstream. This is seen especially in people who use intravenous drugs, where bacteria may be spread by dirty needles. Most commonly an abscess comes from an infection in another part of the body, such as a sinus infection, dental abscess, or tuberculosis. Bacteria may enter through an opening in the brain when a bullet, some other object, or a surgeon penetrates the skull. There are other causes, too.

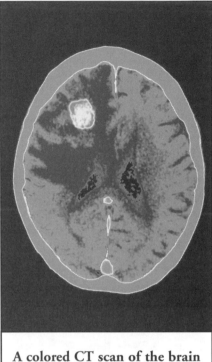

A colored CT scan of the brain of a person with AIDS shows an abscess (upper left).

A brain abscess that is caused by bacteria can be treated with antibiotics. In some cases, the pus of an abscess is removed surgically by puncturing the center of the lesion. A brain abscess that is left untreated can cause pressure and spread infection, causing the death of brain cells, and even the whole body.

Meningitis

Meningitis is the inflammation of the membranes that cover the brain and spinal cord. There are a number of different types. Meningitis can be caused by viruses, bacteria, fungi, and the organism that causes tuberculosis. At any time, one in ten people will be carrying, in the lining of their noses and in their throats, the bacteria that can cause meningococcal meningitis. In a relatively few people, the bacteria overcome the body's immune system and pass through the linings of the nose and throat into the bloodstream.

Someone with meningitis will become ill very rapidly. Symptoms include a severe headache, vomiting, a high fever, dislike of bright lights, and drowsiness. A doctor should be contacted immediately if this disease is suspected. Some cases are short lived but in others, the disease progresses so rapidly that death occurs during the first forty-eight hours. When someone in a school is diagnosed with meningitis caused by bacteria, classmates are quickly treated with antibiotics.

The development of vaccines has led to a large drop in cases of some kinds of meningitis. The disease is rare, striking about 2,600 people in the United States per year. When more than a few children are affected in one area, an inoculation program may be started. A vaccine is effective only when given well in advance of exposure to the kind of meningitis it prevents. When an epidemic appears to be developing, a large number of people may be vaccinated.[19]

Encephalitis

Encephalitis is a broad term used to cover many kinds of infections in the brain that cause severe inflammation and swelling. The effects are sometimes mild but may be severe, causing permanent brain damage or a condition in which the brain dies first.

Encephalitis may be caused by a virus carried by a mosquito or a tick, or by a virus that is ingested or inhaled. One group of viruses that causes encephalitis infects the gastrointestinal tract. These viruses are discharged in feces and can then be spread by unsanitary food workers who don't wash their hands after using the toilet. Encephalitis may be caused by other types of viruses, such as herpesvirus, mumps virus, HIV, and adenoviruses.

In 1999 an outbreak of encephalitis occurred in the New York City area. It was first thought to be St. Louis encephalitis. Later it was learned that the disease was caused by a West Nile virus. This form of encephalitis had never been detected in the Western Hemisphere. It is spread by mosquitoes from birds–especially crows–to people. St Louis and West Nile viruses cause the same type of disease, but there are slight differences in the form of the brain damage.

AIDS dementia (HIV encephalopathy) affects between 20 and 30 percent of all AIDS patients. This complication may be due to infection of brain tissue or abnormal immune responses to toxoplasmosis and other kinds of infection.[20] As with other dementias, forgetfulness, inability to concentrate, poor judgment, personality change, and slowed thinking signal the early

41

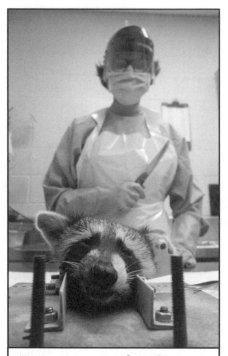

To test a raccoon for rabies, a researcher must remove some brain tissue from the animal's head.

stage of AIDS dementia. Speech and thinking deteriorate and patients become bedridden, paralyzed, and mute. In AIDS, the immune system is weakened, and other infectious diseases may also appear, compounding the problems of dementia.

Rabies

Rabies is an acute viral infection of the brain and spinal cord, usually spread through the bite of an infected animal. Rabies virus travels quickly to the nerve nearest the bite and continues on nerve pathways to the brain. It multiplies there and eventually travels to the salivary glands. Immediate treatment can prevent the infection from spreading to the central nervous system, but if it does spread, the disease is almost always fatal. Rabies has been called hydrophobia (fear of water) because in about half the number of affected people, water causes painful throat-muscle spasms. Eventually, even the thought of water causes uncontrollable muscle spasms and excessive saliva that dribbles from the mouth.

Most people are aware of laws requiring rabies vaccinations for cats and dogs. These laws help protect human beings from rabies by forming a barrier to the spread of rabies from wild animals. However, not everyone realizes that rabies is caused by a virus that can infect all warm-blooded mammals. Rabid animals are usually either vicious and aggressive or appear to be partially

42

or totally paralyzed. Some appear to be drunk. Some animals spread the disease even though they appear to be normal.

It is especially important to avoid contact with all bats, raccoons, skunks, groundhogs, and foxes since rabid animals are prone to biting and scratching. Stray cats and dogs may not have been vaccinated, so they, too, may be carriers. Any contact with these animals should be reported to a doctor. If there is any suspicion of rabies, medical treatment should be sought at once. Animals who are suspected of rabies are quarantined whenever possible. They may have to be killed so that their brain tissue may be analyzed for the rabies virus since this is the way to reach a definitive diagnosis.

Toxoplasmosis

Except for many AIDS patients and other immunosuppressed people, such as those who have transplants or are being treated for cancer, toxoplasma lives harmlessly in the bodies of 20 to 70 percent of Americans.[20] This protozoan, the one-celled animal called *Toxoplasma gondii,* is easily spread by contact with contaminated soil or cat litter. Since litter does not become infected until one to four days after an infected cat uses the litter box, changing litter daily will prevent the spread of toxoplasmosis. The disease can also be spread by flies, by ingesting meat that is not properly cooked, or eating food that is contaminated by feces.

Toxoplasmosis is especially dangerous for pregnant women who are not immune. If it is acquired in the first trimester, babies are often stillborn. About one-third of the infected babies who survive are born with toxoplasmosis. They may have "water on the brain" (hydrocephalus), abnormally small heads, or other defects. Months or years later, children may develop blindness, epilepsy, or mental retardation from the infection. In adults, the disease may be mild, or it may cause delirium, seizures, encephalitis, and other problems.

There are numerous infectious diseases of the brain, and many of them cause dementia. The search continues for ways to prevent the death of the brain by infection.

CHAPTER FIVE

Alzheimer's Disease: The Mystery of Vanishing Minds

Sixteen-year-old Beth asks, "What can I do when my grand-mother insists on going to visit her sister Mary?" Mary died five years ago. Beth's grandmother has Alzheimer's disease. By tomorrow, or perhaps in the next hour, she will forget about wanting to see Mary.

Alzheimer's disease is a progressive, irreversible, downhill slide into brain death. Once considered a rare disorder, it is now recognized as the most common cause of dementia and a major health problem.

Many elderly people fear that they are in the early stages of this disease. Tessa's grandmother thinks she is getting Alzheimer's every time she misplaces something. Whenever Bernard cannot remember a name, he asks, "Am I getting Alzheimer's?" While most people's fears are unfounded, Alzheimer's disease does affect about 4 million people in the United States. As many as 30 to 50 percent of people over the age of eighty-five have it. (This is a rough estimate since dif-ferent surveys use different criteria and many people are unwilling to participate in surveys about dementia.) It seems certain that after the age of sixty-five the percentage of those affected approximately doubles with every decade of life.[1]

Alzheimer's disease is not "just old age." About 10 to 30 percent of people over the age of sixty-five maintain high lev-els of mental functioning. A middle group includes people who function moderately well intellectually, but have enough difficulty with memory to find it annoying. The remaining group is made up of people who suffer from diseases that lead to dementia. Most people still attribute the loss of mental function in the elderly to aging rather than to disease, and even doctors fail to recognize early Alzheimer's and other kinds of dementia in their patients 75 percent of the time.[2] Researchers are working desperately to find a cure for this disease, which steals the minds of so many men and women over a long and devastating period of time.

Living with Alzheimer's

Eighty-year-old Don was experiencing some of the problems of a person suffering from Alzheimer's. There were days when Don showed no symptoms, but on most days he had periods of difficulty. On Monday, Don banged his head against the bedroom wall at rapid intervals for about five minutes. His wife, Sara, watched, wishing she could help him.

On Tuesday, Don had an especially difficult time expressing himself. Some words came out twisted, while others were inappropriate. Sara tried to treat their conversations as puzzles, but Don's impatience at her lack of understanding made this difficult.

On Wednesday, Don wandered off when it was time for a doctor's appointment. This behavior was not unusual, for he frequently wandered away, and he could no longer tell time correctly. Dressing was often a problem, especially when he had to go out. One particular day his sweater was on backwards, his pants were inside-out, and his shoes did not match. If Sara suggested that he change his clothing, he felt she was criticizing him, so she ignored most situations that were not dangerous.

The whole week, and every week, there were incidents that frustrated Don and his wife. Sometimes they were simple things like finding the jelly in a drawer, but other times there were lost messages on the answering machine, or broken and lost treasures. It was hard, also, to help grown children and grandchildren to understand Don's behavior.

Don knew he was developing Alzheimer's disease (AD), and he was aware of would happen in the future. He lived in a retirement community with a health center where several friends in more advanced stages of the disease lived. At the center, Don's friend Dave, a retired surgeon, "made rounds" each morning, believing that he was still a practicing physician at the hospital. Fred, Dave's roommate, had been an especially gentle and polite man before he developed Alzheimer's. Now he was aggressive. He chased some women patients down the hall and threatened them with a table knife. Most of the time he needed to be subdued by medication. Don often threatened to kill himself rather than go to the health center as his disease grew worse.

Each day was different for Don, as it is for other Alzheimer's patients. In time, memory fails, the ability to understand new things decreases, and it is difficult to carry on a conversation. It becomes harder to find the words, or even remember the beginning of a sentence. People with Alzheimer's eventually need help dressing, bathing, and eating. They may become angry and suspicious for no apparent reason, may accuse others of stealing, and may act inappropriately in public. Each case is different, but many people with AD suffer from depression.

What Happens in the Brain?

In people with Alzheimer's disease, plaques and tangles accumulate in the brain, causing neurons to die. The plaques have a core made of a substance known as amyloid protein and are surrounded by what looks like a halo of damaged axons, and dendrites. The tangles contain fragments of protein from fibers that are common to nerve cells. These may be debris from wounded brain cells or part of the process of destruction. No one really knows.

The progression in Alzheimer's is the reverse of normal maturation. Babies learn to swallow, then to smile at caregivers. They begin to vocalize and to repeat words. They start crawling and then walk. Gradually verbal skills improve, and

Cerebral cortex: involved in conscious thought and language.

Basal forebrain: has large numbers of neurons containing acetylcholine, a chemical important in memory and learning.

Hippocampus: essential to memory storage. The earliest signs of Alzheimer's are found in the nearby entorhinal cortex (not shown).

Neuritic plaques

Neurofibrillary tangles

Neuron

Hallmarks of Alzeimer's disease include neuritic plaques (outside neurons), and neurofibrillary tangles (inside neurons).

© National Institutes of Health

The brain and Alzheimer's disease: Alzheimer's disease attacks nerve cells (neurons) in several regions of the brain.

toddlers learn bowel and bladder control. In the next few years, memory improves and judgment develops. With Alzheimer's, this sequence is reversed. Verbal skills, understanding, and memory decrease. Eventually, patients are unable to talk and walk, and even to swallow. They become incontinent and lack the ability to care for themselves.[3] How early these and other changes occur varies from one individual to another.

Coping with the Stigma

Sixteen-year-old Tina and her grandmother had always had a close relationship. When Tina had an unwanted pregnancy, her grandmother helped her through the difficult time. When Tina noted that her grandmother was becoming confused, she tried to help by spending more time with her, taking her to the doctor, managing her finances, and shopping for her.

Once her grandmother embarrassed Tina in front of her friends by strange remarks. When Tina sought help from her school counselor, he suggested that she join a support group for teens. Local chapters of the Alzheimer's Association are listed in the phone book, and they provide a variety of such services. At the support group Tina learned how to cope with some of the things her grandmother did. She became more comfortable about explaining Alzheimer's as a disease to her friends. They were more understanding when they knew that AD affects the brain, killing neurons, so that people become confused, unable to express themselves clearly, and unable, eventually, to care for themselves.

Tina's mother, Jane, who was the main caregiver, found it helpful to share her feelings with her daughter. This was especially true when the grandmother's accusations of neglect and hate made Jane feel that she was not appreciated. Tina could remind her mother that angry and violent behavior were a result of the disease affecting her grandmother's brain. Tina's grandmother was anxious because she did not always know where she was or what she was expected to do. Together, Jane and Tina struggled with the difficult times experienced by millions of people who care for loved ones suffering from Alzheimer's and other kinds of dementia.

Is It Really Alzheimer's?

There is no specific test for Alzheimer's disease, but a doctor can rule out other possible reasons for symptoms. Tests may include an electrocardiogram (the pattern of electroactivity of heart muscles), urinalysis, CT scan (a computerized scan or image of the brain), blood tests, interviews with a neurologist, and written psychological tests. Ninety percent of the time, Alzheimer's is identified correctly in the early stages. The only certain diagnosis can be made after a person's death, through an examination of the brain tissue to determine if the typical plaques and tangles are present.

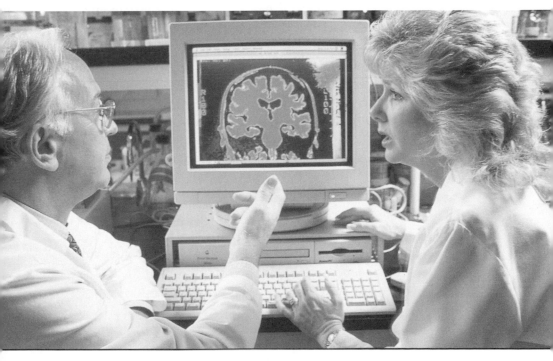

Researchers discuss the MRI of the brain of an Alzheimer's patient while viewing it on a computer screen.

Depression, multiple minor strokes, hormonal deficiency, exposure to environmental toxins and allergy-causing substances, excessive alcohol drinking, and other damaging habits can contribute to conditions that mimic early Alzheimer's.

An Ancient Disease

Ancient Greek and Roman writers described symptoms similar to those recognized as Alzheimer's disease today. In the sixteenth century, Shakespeare wrote about very old age as a time of "second childishness and mere oblivion," suggesting that symptoms of Alzheimer's or something similar were known and recognized then. In the early 1900s, a German psychiatrist, Alois Alzheimer, reported the case of a woman who had severe memory impairment and other symptoms that are now recognized as part of the disease that carries his name. Between 1970 and 1980, autopsies of brains from severely demented patients indicated the presence of many plaques and tangles.[4]

Searching for Causes

In their search for causes of this disease, scientists have discovered that many factors are involved, and they probably interact differently in different patients. In some cases, there are genetic links. For example, people who inherit a gene that directs the production of a variant of apolipoprotein E4 (ApoE4) appear to be at risk for developing Alzheimer's disease. No one knows for sure why some of the people who carry this gene develop AD and some do not.[5] Many genes may be involved.

In 1995 two genetic abnormalities that are associated with early-onset Alzheimer's were identified. This form of the disease affects people forty to fifty years old and almost always runs in families. It accounts for about 10 percent of all cases of AD.[6]

Clues to the cause of AD may lie in the complex signaling system of the brain. The concentration of a neurotransmitter called acetylcholine falls sharply in people with the disease, and it is known that this chemical is critical in the process of forming memories. Acetylcholine has been the

Former President Ronald Reagan—shown here with Nancy Reagan at his eighty-third birthday party in 1994—is one of the prominent people who are known to suffer from Alzheimer's.

focus of hundreds of studies.[7] Reduced levels of other neurotransmitters are implicated, too.

Scientists are also studying toxic chemicals, problems with bodily systems that turn food into energy, and the shapes and actions of the nerve cells. They are looking at the role of the immune system in producing antibodies against its own cells. Some researchers suggest a slow virus, one that can lie dormant in the body for many years, as a possible cause. Investigations to find such a virus are underway, but have yielded little hard evidence.

An exciting discovery in the search for causes of Alzheimer's was announced in the fall of 1999 when scientists confirmed they had found the enzyme, beta-secretase. This enzyme snips a protein that protrudes from brain cells, leading to the release of toxic fragments. Scientists believe the discovery opens the door to the development of drugs that might stop the progress of the disease or prevent it in those at risk.[8]

Risk Factors

"How can I avoid Alzheimer's?" is a question without any definite answer. Some head injuries may be a factor, since it is possible that concussions might later influence the onset of Alzheimer's.

Excessive cortisol production may be a cause of the death of brain cells. Stress increases the amount of this hormone which is produced in the adrenal glands.[9] Although stress is probably not a root cause of AD, it could be a factor that nudges the disease toward faster brain death. Ways to avoid or cope with stress are described in many books available at libraries.

Low educational level may increase the risk for AD. Research suggests that the more years of formal education a person has completed, the less likely he or she is to develop Alzheimer's.[10] Low linguistic ability in early life may be a subtle symptom of very early changes in the brain that ultimately lead to AD.[11] Some other risk factors that are being investigated include Down's syndrome, cardiovascular disease, the action of estrogen (a hormone) and nerve growth factor, a history of high alcohol consumption, hypothyroidism (an undersecretion of the thyroid hormone), and a long history of depression. As mentioned earlier, age and family history are well-known risk factors.

Scientists are trying to unravel the mystery of AD through many approaches. Some work toward understanding causes, others search for meaningful treatments, and others look for better ways to diagnose the disease. Early diagnosis, or predicting the disease in advance, might play an important role in slowing, or even stopping, the course of degeneration. The rapid pace of research has shed much light on AD, and many neuroscientists think that a means to prevent or treat Alzheimer's will be found in the foreseeable future.

CHAPTER SIX

Parkinson's, Huntington's, and Other Degenerative Diseases

Alzheimer's disease is the most common cause of dementia, but it is certainly not the only one. And while most diseases that lead to dementia appear in the later years of life, sometimes the brain dies first—in the bodies of children.

Batten Disease

Caitlin became blind at the age of seven. She developed seizures, which became more frequent each year. By the time she was fifteen, so many of her brain cells had died that she suffered from severe dementia. Two years later, she died. Caitlin had Batten disease, a neurodegenerative disorder that strikes about one baby in 25,000.[1]

Batten disease is a fatal, inherited disorder of the nervous system. The symptoms begin to appear early in childhood. In some cases, the early signs are subtle: slow learning, clumsiness or stumbling, personality and behaviorial changes. Over time, there is loss of sight and motor skills, worsening seizures, and mental impairment. The disease is often fatal by the late teens or early twenties.

Batten disease in not contagious, and at this time, it is not preventable. It is the juvenile form of the disease NCL (neuronal ceroid lipofuscinosis), in which certain fats and pigments build up in cells of the brain, eyes, and many other tissues.

Research into the genetic cause of Batten disease is supported by the National Institute of Neurological Disorders and

Stroke (NINDS), which conducts studies of the brain and spinal cord. In addition, the institute works with animal models, such as sheep or mice, to improve understanding and treatment of Batten disease. Some families donate the brains of patients who have died of Batten disease in order to help researchers learn more about the disease.

Multiple Sclerosis

About 350,000 to 500,000 Americans suffer from multiple sclerosis (MS), a disease of the nervous system that typically begins between the late teens and fifty. MS is unpredictable in course and extent, but it involves the transmission of messages between the nervous system and the rest of the body. Multiple sclerosis can affect the brain, spinal cord, and peripheral nerves (the sensory or motor neurons connecting the surface of the body with the central nervous system). People with multiple sclerosis often suffer from optic neuritis, an inflammation of the optic nerve. This disease can produce red-green colorblindness and even the loss of sight in the affected eye.

People with multiple sclerosis also tend to suffer from extreme fatigue. In addition to difficulty walking, many have problems in bowel and bladder control and have slurred speech, poor vision, and some loss of mental functions. The symptoms usually become worse with time. Understandably, people with MS often become depressed.

Vernon's first symptoms of multiple sclerosis included optic neuritis and some muscle weakness. By the time he was a senior in high school, the gradual loss of strength in his arms and legs had made it difficult for him to walk. He felt tired and complained of numbness and tingling in his arms and legs. Vernon's future looked grim, but in the last decade there has been a great deal of research into MS, and advances in diagnosis and therapy. Several new drugs are under study.

MS may be an autoimmune disease—one in which cells that are charged with ridding the body of foreign substances turn on the body's own tissues. A main cause of the symp-

Since former Mousekeeter and performer Annette Funicello was diagnosed with multiple sclerosis, she has worked to increase public understanding of the disease. Here, flanked by Minnie and Mickey Mouse, she is honored for her efforts.

toms of multiple sclerosis is the loss of some of the material that insulates nerve cells, a fatty sheath known as myelin. One theory suggests that MS is the result of an earlier infection, such as the childhood viral disease, roseola. Long after the symptoms of the disease have disappeared, some immune system cells may be roused against the roseola virus that remains dormant in nerve cells and may attack the myelin.

In addition to the loss of myelin, there may be other causes of MS symptoms. In a recent study, scientists using a laser-scanning microscope observed the severing of some nerve cells in the brains of patients with MS.[2] This discovery may lead to new therapies for MS and other diseases.

Lewy Body Dementia

Helen seemed perfectly well much of the time, but now and then she showed some symptoms that made her doctor wonder if she had Parkinson's disease. After a while, she became confused. Sometimes she said she could see her husband in the corner of the room, and each time he appeared in the same corner. Since he had died ten years earlier, this was a visual hallucination.

Helen's doctor discovered that she suffered from Lewy body dementia, a disease with many of the same symptoms as Alzheimer's—progressive loss of memory, language, reasoning, and other higher mental functions. The progress of Lewy body dementia may be more rapid than that of Alzheimer's, and it is often combined with Alzheimer's or Parkinson's disease. Abnormal brain cells, called cortical Lewy bodies, are distributed through the brains of people with Lewy body dementia. Although there is no cure for this disease, it is sometimes possible to treat some of the symptoms with medication.

Pick's Disease

Charlotte's mother lost her job as a producer at the local television network because she became very angry and unpredictable day after day. Examinations revealed that she suffered from Pick's disease, a progressively degenerative disease similar to Alzheimer's. Pick's disease, however, produces different abnormalities in the cells of the brain. For example, round, microscopic structures, known as Pick bodies, are found upon examination of the brain.

Howard's short attention span and his confusion about where he was were the early signs of his disease. Previously, Howard had spent long periods of time on his watercolor painting, but now he would get out the materials, paint for a few minutes, and walk away. Personality change is one of the first symptoms of Pick's disease. Before his disease developed, Howard was thin and very careful about his diet. Now, he wanted to eat everything in sight and he gained so much weight that he needed new clothes every few months. He had no idea that there was anything wrong with him, but his doctor explained that the frontal lobe of his brain was deteriorating.

Families struggling with a loved one who has Pick's disease can share their problems and support each other in local groups and on the Internet. Reading about another caregiver whose parent is very possessive of personal things, refuses to bathe, and dislikes having clothing or dishes washed helps someone facing similar problems.

Many caregivers share their concerns about the cost of medicines and nursing homes that may be needed when the patient can no longer be managed at home. They also speak about the tragedy of people with once-brilliant minds who can no longer make simple decisions, speak, or take care of daily functions.

Huntington's Disease

The memory of Woody Guthrie, a well-loved folk singer, lives on in the songs and tributes of his son Arlo Guthrie, and Bob Dylan, Joan Baez, and other popular folk singers who admired him. Woody Guthrie's career was interrupted when he developed symptoms of Huntington's disease, an illness that was not commonly recognized in 1963. When Bob Dylan visited Woody Guthrie in his hospital bed that year in Brooklyn, New York, *Time* magazine reported that Woody was terribly ill "with a nervous disease."[3] Not everyone knew that this was Huntington's disease, a devastating, progressive disorder of the brain that leads to uncontrollable movements, loss of intellectual faculties, and emotional problems. Unfortunately there is still no cure for this inherited disease that affects about 25,000 people in the United States.

Huntington's disease was first recognized and described in America in 1848. It was later given the name Huntington's chorea, based on a famous description of the disease by George Huntington in 1910. "Chorea" is the Greek word for dancing, and refers to the uncontrollable shaking that is symptomatic of the disease. Today, it is known as Huntington's disease or HD. George Huntington described it as follows:

The popular folk singer Woody Guthrie, seen in a photograph from the late 1930s, developed Huntington's disease, an inherited disease that affects the nervous system.

The hereditary chorea...is confined to certain and fortunately a few families, and has been transmitted to them, an heirloom from generations away back in the distant past. It is spoken of by those in whose brain the seeds of the disease are known to exist with a kind of horror, and not at all alluded to except through dire necessity...When either or both parents have shown manifestations of the disease, one or more of the offspring almost invariably suffer from the disease, if they live to an adult age; but if by any chance these children go through life without it, the thread is broken, and the grandchildren or great grandchildren of the original shakers may rest assured that they are free from the disease...Unstable and whimsical as the disease may be in other respects, in this it is firm, it never skips a generation to manifest itself in another...[4]

Today, the pattern of inheritance of Huntington's disease as a dominant trait is well known. Each child of an affected parent has a 50 percent chance of inheriting the disease, and one who inherits the abnormal gene has a 50 percent chance of passing it along to the next generation. If the gene is present, symptoms usually develop between the ages of thirty and fifty, although they can start earlier or later.

Since symptoms of HD do not usually develop until after a person reaches child-bearing age, some young people who think they might carry the abnormal gene choose to have genetic testing. Others prefer not to know. However, people at risk for HD who are not tested may find themselves spending much time searching for the first signs of the disease. They may worry every time they drop a plate, are in a bad mood, or forget a name.

The illness begins gradually, with changes caused by the loss of cells in two areas of the brain. This damage to the brain affects thinking, judgment, memory, movement, and emotional control. After symptoms begin, there is a downhill course of increasing emotional disturbances and disability in walking and other movements. Unusual movements of the limbs, such as purposeless flicks of an arm or leg appear in the early stages. The movements are involuntary but they may be actively suppressed for very short periods of time.

Symptoms vary widely from person to person, and may include depression, anxiety, apathy, facial grimaces, twisting, and excessive restlessness. Later there may be almost constant movement with stretching and twisting, accompanied by guttural noises. By five to fifteen years after the symptoms begin, constant thrashing movements of the body cease only during sleep.

Scientists have isolated the gene for HD and have been able to breed mice that developed symptoms of the disease. The mice developed severe problems with walking and lost weight, just as people with HD do. Scientists have also discovered that cell death in HD may be caused by a ball of protein that forms in the nucleus of certain cells in the brain.[5] Some researchers believe that experimental surgery using fetal tissue implants and gene therapy offer promising avenues of research. Doctors are making strides in relieving the symptoms, and there is hope that uncovering new pieces of the puzzle will result in the prevention of and ability to cure HD.

Parkinson's Disease

Over a million people in the United States suffer from Parkinson's disease (PD). Although most of them are over fifty years old, there is also a form that strikes teenagers.[6] Victims often resemble the comedian Charlie Chaplin, with stooped posture and a shuffling gait. In Parkinson's disease, certain cells in the brain deteriorate, reducing the supply of the neurotransmitter dopamine. The primary symptoms include tremor, stiffness, and difficulty with movement, including walking, and balance. Some victims suffer from depression and have difficulty speaking and other symptoms. In most cases the symptoms are physical, not mental, but dementia can be one of them.

Although the causes of PD are unknown, some cases occurred after the viral influenza encephalitis epidemic in the

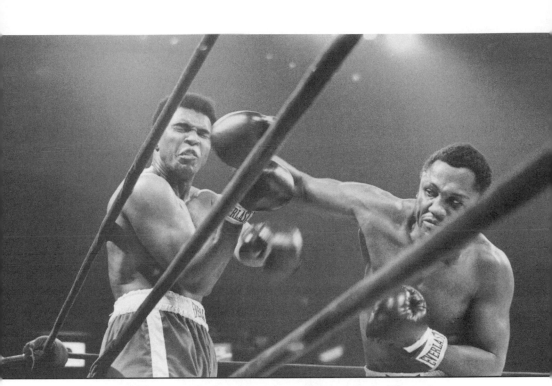
Repeated blows to the head may cause brain injury. The prize-fighter Muhammad Ali (left), wincing from the impact of Joe Frazier's punch, now suffers from Parkinson's disease.

early nineteen hundreds. Illegal drug use has induced parkinsonian symptoms in a number of young people after they used MPTP, a drug that is related to the narcotic painkiller Demerol.

Parkinson's disease is caused by a gradual loss of cells in the area of the brain known as the substantia nigra. This term means "black substance," and this part of the brain is pigmented. It normally produces the chemical dopamine, which it distributes to another portion of the brain known as the stratium. The stratium is the coordination center for various brain circuits, and when there is insufficient dopamine, the chemical imbalance leads to symptoms of Parkinson's.

As the cells in these two areas of the brain are damaged, cells in other parts of the brain may take over the production of dopamine, but eventually they fail. Other neurotransmitters are involved in the disease, too. Parkinson's disease has been described as one of the most baffling and complex of the neurological disorders.[7]

In 1817, James Parkinson, a British physician, published a short book called *An Essay on the Shaking Palsy*, in which he described the symptoms of the disease that bears his name. The fundamental brain defect, the loss of dopamine, was not identified until 1960, and this led to the first successful treatment. However, much about the disease remains a mystery. Doctors still don't know what causes the loss of the brain cells or how to cure the disease.[8]

Finding the right combination of drugs to control the symptoms of PD is often difficult. The most common drug treatment is levodopa (L-dopa), a medicine that converts to dopamine in the brain. Another drug, carbidopa, is widely used to supplement the levodopa. Medicines are credited with increasing the life span of people with Parkinson's by five years. About one third of people with PD respond to levodopa all their lives, but for others the effect wears off between doses.[9]

Sandra's symptoms began five years ago, and they had been fairly well controlled by levodopa. The side effects of the levodopa included involuntary movements, but Sandra coped with that. However, in recent months, she has fluctuated between periods in which she can move smoothly and times when her movements are slow and the tremors return. Sometimes, when she gets up after sitting, her feet seem frozen in place for as long as five minutes. And sometimes, after taking her medication, her arms and legs flail about uncontrollably as an oversensitive response to her medication. She has tried many other medications for PD but none have been helpful. She asked her doctor about surgery that had helped a friend. Unfortunately, she was not a candidate for this surgery because she was already exhibiting signs of dementia.

Bill was a better candidate for surgery. His symptoms began twenty years ago and he had been helped by many combinations of medicine, but they were no longer preventing symptoms. He retired from his teaching job at the university and gave up driving his car and piloting his plane. He still managed to do research on the Internet at home to keep his mind active, but now he had great difficulty just walking from one side of the room to the other. His hand shook so badly that he could barely drink his morning coffee. As his condition worsened, his doctor suggested an operation known as pallidotomy.

Pallidotomy is a type of surgery that has been performed since the 1940s, but it was not then as precise as it is today. Some patients improved, some did not, and some died. In the 1960s, doctors largely abandoned this operation in favor of effective new drugs. Today, with more sophisticated techniques, the operation is being performed on a limited number of people, like Bill, who are no longer helped by medicine or have severe side effects from it. Although the risks are less than they were in 1940s, they are still serious.

Early in 1995, viewers of "60 Minutes," "Prime Time Live," and other television programs saw people who suffered from PD leaving operating rooms liberated from the terrible jerking and rigidity that had controlled their lives. These programs led to a fierce demand for pallidotomies. But doctors still had questions about the procedure's effects and safety. They are still questioning whether or not the benefits are lasting.[10]

Bill was willing to accept the risks of the surgery, and his doctor agreed. During Bill's operation, a group of cells deep in the brain were accessed through a small hole in his skull. He was awake while the doctor explored different areas of his brain in an effort to locate the exact place that was causing the problem. Bill's head was held in place by a stereotactic frame—a three-sided metal frame with coordinates—to help position the probe. These coordinates were determined in advance through a series of brain scans. The frame held a long, heated wire in place as it was passed into his brain, and the designated area was explored one millimeter at a time. When the exact position was located, the tiny tip of the wire destroyed the target cells.[11] After this tissue was destroyed, Bill's symptoms were relieved.

Finding the exact spot for destruction of tissue in a pallidotomy can be difficult. If surgeons do not feel that they have found the exact target, they do not proceed. They do not burn someone's brain without knowing exactly where they are.[12] The operation is a very serious one. Strokes, vision loss, or some other less serious complications may result. It is usually performed only on one side of the brain, since destroying tissue on both sides is even riskier.

Why can destroying more tissue help when the problem is that cells have are already been destroyed? This is difficult to understand. One explanation suggests that the disease interrupts connections to parts of the brain that control certain activities, such as a tendency to be spastic or rigid. These connections inhibit the activity, and thus enable the body to function normally. Surgery can restore the necessary balance.

With sophisticated new brain imaging and mapping techniques, many pallidotomies yield impressive results, but the operation is not appropriate for everyone. Most experts estimate that only about 5 to 10 percent of the million Americans with Parkinson's disease might be good candidates for pallidotomy.[13] In addition to people like Sandra who have developed dementia, those who never responded well to medications in the first place, those who are quite old, or those who have tremors as their main symptom are not candidates for this kind of surgery.

Another approach to helping people with PD is the use of a brain "pacemaker." In this procedure, a thin wire is implanted in a certain part of the brain (thalamus) and is connected to a stimulator similar to a heart pacemaker that is implanted near the collarbone. Brain tissue is not destroyed in this operation and tremors may be controlled as a result of the implanting of the "pacemaker."

In another form of treatment, some doctors are attempting to replace damaged nerve cells with healthy cells to compensate for the loss. Cells capable of producing dopamine come

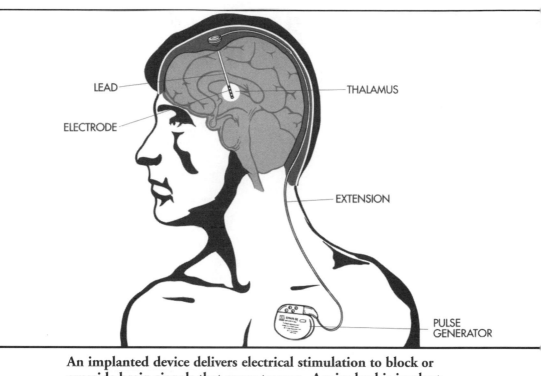

LEAD

ELECTRODE

THALAMUS

EXTENSION

PULSE
GENERATOR

An implanted device delivers electrical stimulation to block or override brain signals that cause tremor. A wire lead is implanted in the brain and stimulates target nuclei in the thalamus. An extension connects it to a pulse generator implanted near the collarbone.

from a gland above the kidney (the adrenal medulla), or from aborted fetuses, or are genetically engineered.[14]

Each case is different, and what helps in one case may not help in another. Researchers are still exploring many fronts in efforts to prevent and treat Huntington's disease, Parkinson's disease, and other degenerative diseases in which parts of the brain die first.

CHAPTER SEVEN

Brain Death by Stroke and Vascular Dementia

Like a human-made computer, the brain is capable of incredible feats of memory, coordination, and organization, all while requiring a constant but very small amount of energy for proper operation. Yet unlike other human organs that can survive for hours or days without fuel, the sensitive cells of the brain are permanently damaged after only five minutes without oxygen and glucose, a form of sugar.

An intricate system of blood vessels furnishes fuel to the brain. These vessels, the arteries, are arranged in a branching pattern like a tree. The trunk leads to large branches, then to smaller branches, and ultimately to twigs visible only by microscope. Large arteries, each about the thickness of a pencil, arise from the great vessels near the heart and pass through the neck to reach the brain. These channels, called carotid and vertebral arteries, divide into smaller and smaller passages until microscopic capillaries finally touch individual brain cells. There the blood circulation trades oxygen and fresh nutrients for carbon dioxide and other waste products produced by the brain cells.

When a Brain Attack Occurs

When a region of the brain is permanently denied oxygen and nourishment, the function carried out by that region is weakened or vanishes completely. This can happen when a stroke, or brain attack, occurs. The stroke might cause weakness on one side of the body, loss of speech or understanding, problems

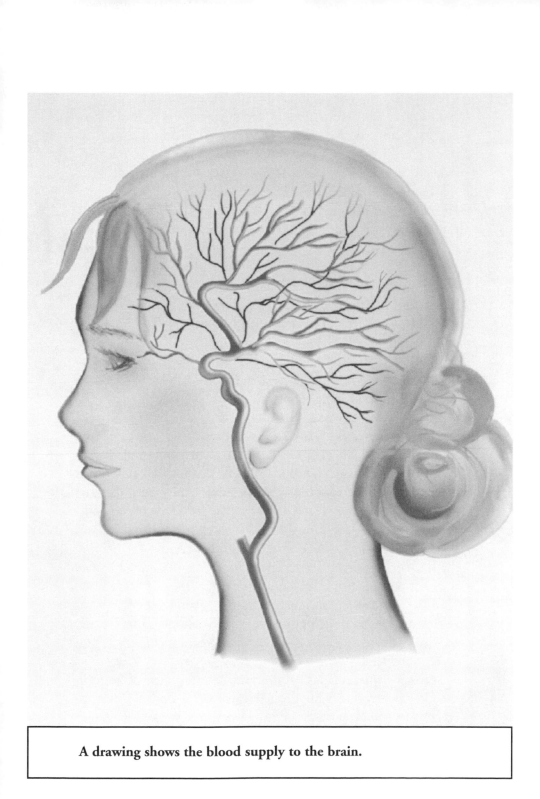

A drawing shows the blood supply to the brain.

with swallowing food, inability to read or see, mental confusion, lack of physical coordination, or loss of emotional control. If loss of blood flow, or ischemia, is temporary and brain function returns within twenty-four hours, the diagnosis is transient ischemic attack (TIA). As used here, transient means passing.

David's grandfather seemed to be doing well two months after a serious heart attack. He was looking forward to leaving the hospital and returning to his gardening and other activities. He was ready to follow his doctor's advice to quit smoking, reduce his blood fat content (cholesterol), limit the amount of salt in his diet to lower blood pressure, and get his blood sugar under control. It was a lot to tackle all at once, but the seventy-year-old retired truck driver was glad to be alive and happy to make a new start.

One day, after he had returned home, he asked David to help him plant some seedlings after school. While they were in the garden, David noticed something strange: his right-handed grandfather was reaching for objects with his left hand only. After a few minutes, David's grandfather could not move the right side of his body at all and began losing his power of speech. David remained calm and called 911. At the hospital, physicians diagnosed a stroke affecting the left side of the brain, the part that governs speech and movement of the right side of the body. A CT (computerized tomography) scan showed that there was no bleeding in the brain and ruled out other conditions, helping the doctors decide on treatment. This was done quickly, since the treatment had to be given within three hours of the stroke. David's grandfather was given tissue plasminogen activator (TPA), a strong blood-clot dissolving medication. Within hours, the clot that was blocking a crucial brain vessel melted away and he regained all of his faculties.

Stroke, or brain attack, is the third leading cause of death in the United States and the greatest cause of nervous system disability. Many patients and doctors view a large stroke with major disability as a condition worse than death. David's grandfather was fortunate to receive prompt state-of-the-art diagnosis and treatment for his brain attack. Many recoveries are not this complete.

Over one-half million Americans experience a new or second stroke each year, translating into a stroke every minute in the United States.[1] One-third of stroke survivors will have another attack within five years, and four out of five American families will be affected by stroke. Each year stroke costs the United States $30 billion.[2] On a worldwide basis, stroke is a leading cause of death. The problem is likely to worsen in the years ahead because of the growth and aging of the planet's population and the lifestyle changes that come with rising prosperity.

Is There More Than One Type of Stroke?

Loss of blood supply to part of the brain can be caused by one of several types of problems. David's grandfather had an ischemic stroke caused by a thromboembolism. As the doctors

In this drawing, an embolism (blockage), a cause of stroke, is seen (center) in a cerebral artery. The embolism is usually caused by a blood clot.

explained it to David, a thromboembolism means that a blood clot (or thrombus) migrated (or embolized) through the circulatory system and lodged in a brain artery where it stopped the flow of blood. This sort of stroke can occur in a person of any age if that person has a disease of the valves, muscle, or rhythm of the heart that can make the blood stagnate and lead to the formation of clots. Young patients with certain forms of heart-valve disease that follow a bout of rheumatic fever are particularly at risk for thromboembolic stroke. People can also have a tendency toward thromboembolic stroke because of disorders caused by blood that is thicker than normal. These disorders can be present at birth or they may develop later in life.

Older patients with degenerative diseases of the large blood vessels may form clots in their circulatory systems. A careful

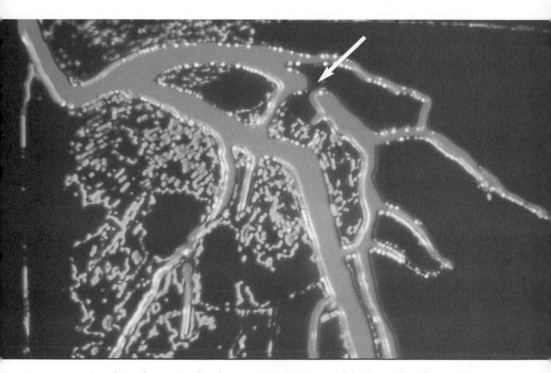

In this photograph of a coronary artery, a blockage can be seen at the upper right, as a gap in the artery.

search for blood clots by ultrasound imaging studies can lead a doctor to recommend blood-thinning treatment as a protective measure against future strokes. In other cases, such as heart rhythm disturbances or the implanting of an artificial metal heart valve, preventive blood-thinning treatment is prescribed as a matter of course. David's grandfather was given a daily blood-thinning tablet, Coumadin (also known as warfarin), to protect against future strokes. This drug therapy requires frequent blood tests to make sure the blood is neither too thick nor dangerously thin. David's grandfather has had no further strokes after he started to take Coumadin pills.

David's grandfather developed a heart attack because of fatty cholesterol-based atherosclerotic blockages in his heart vessels. The same lifestyle factors heightened his risk for carotid and brain artery blockages. Indeed, in his case an ultrasound examination showed partly blocked neck arteries. A stroke caused by fatty cholesterol blockages in the neck or brain artery begins early in life with damage to the delicate layer of cells called the endothelium. These cells, arranged like tiles or paving stones, line the glasslike inner passage of the blood vessel.

The culprits that originally damage the endothelium are still not well known, but several suspects have been suggested. Among physical stresses, high blood pressure may be responsible. The chemical stress of cigarette smoke or high blood sugar concentration, or the biological stress of infection all may play a role as well. As atherosclerotic blockages run in families, inherited or genetic tendencies are almost certainly involved. Once internal vessel damage occurs, white blood cells acting as defenders come to heal the injured artery. But the white blood cells remain at the injured site, burrowing into the vessel wall and feeding on oxidized cholesterol available in the neighboring bloodstream. An atherosclerotic plaque (fatty deposit) then grows, eventually becoming quite large and unstable. Finally the plaque fractures and blood clots form as a natural response to vessel injury. The release of clots and large cholesterol particles into the vessels

71

of the brain causes the vessels downstream to become completely blocked. As a consequence, the brain cells do not receive the necessary fuel and they die.

Plaques are often found in the carotid arteries, but they may also exist in the brain and in the arteries of other body systems. Althea was trying to use exercise as a way to lose weight and quit smoking, but she had to stop her walking program because of severe cramping in her right leg. Her doctor discovered a blocked artery leading to her right leg, which was cleared with medication. One morning Althea awoke with lightheadedness and weakness in her left arm. The feelings passed but she went to see her doctor who told her that she had had a TIA, or transient ischemic attack. An X-ray showed a 99 percent blockage of her right carotid artery. She underwent a surgical operation, called a carotid endarterectomy, in which fatty cholesterol plaque was cleaned out of the vessel under local anesthesia. The operation was a success, and normal blood flow to the brain was restored.

Strokes are more frequent in the early morning, when blood pressure and natural adrenaline are highest and blood anticlotting activity lowest. Smoking and high blood pressure place older people at risk, and high blood cholesterol and high blood sugar (diabetes) are other key factors. Some studies point to the lack of estrogen, a natural hormone, in women who have gone through menopause as another risk factor. Estrogen may help to maintain the resiliency of arteries, helps to keep the endothelium layer intact, and lowers blood pressure and cholesterol content.

Geographically, stroke occurs with greater frequency across the southeastern United States, which is why the region is sometimes called the Stroke Belt. This may be due to a higher concentration of smokers, African-Americans, and elderly people of all ethnic groups, and to local dietary practices, such as high salt and fat consumption.[3]

Some people whose minds deteriorate before their bodies are found to have had multiple small strokes. The cumulative effect of these, through years of advancing blood vessel damage, is a decline in intellectual functioning. This condition is called vascular dementia. Diabetes and untreated hypertension recently were linked to decline in mental functioning,[4] and lack of estrogen in older women may cause similar deterioration.[5]

Ellis was a high school tennis star. By age seventeen, he had filled a shelf with sports trophies and honors. He was a good and popular student, too. One day, while volleying with a practice partner, Ellis complained of an excruciating headache, collapsed suddenly, and became unconscious. After a 911 call, an ambulance took him to the hospital where doctors said he had suffered a hemorrhagic stroke (cerebral hemorrhage or bleeding stroke), another major form of stroke. The cause was a ruptured aneurysm—an inborn weakening in the wall of a major brain blood vessel. Like a time bomb waiting to explode, Ellis's aneurysm had caused no symptoms and he had appeared perfectly healthy. But when the aneurysm burst, a large amount of blood was released under pressure into the closed space of his skull. This caused massive distortion and swelling of the delicate brain tissue. Had the swelling been any more severe, it would have compressed the brain centers that govern breathing and heartbeat and Ellis would have died. Treatments were given to relieve the pressure. Since major brain damage had not occurred, this promising young student athlete has resumed his life. Not all patients do as well.

Some blood vessel problems may run in families and therefore could be detected and perhaps someday even treated using high-tech genetic methods.[6] Other types of hemorrhagic stroke are caused by years of untreated high blood pressure. This type of physical stress leads to weakening in the blood vessel wall. Extremely high blood pressure can even cause brain swelling and coma. Other people may develop hemorrhagic stroke because of long-term alcohol abuse. Blood-thinning treatments, for example aspirin, anticoagulants, or clot-dissolving medications for the prevention or treatment of blood clots, can sometimes lead to hemorrhagic

73

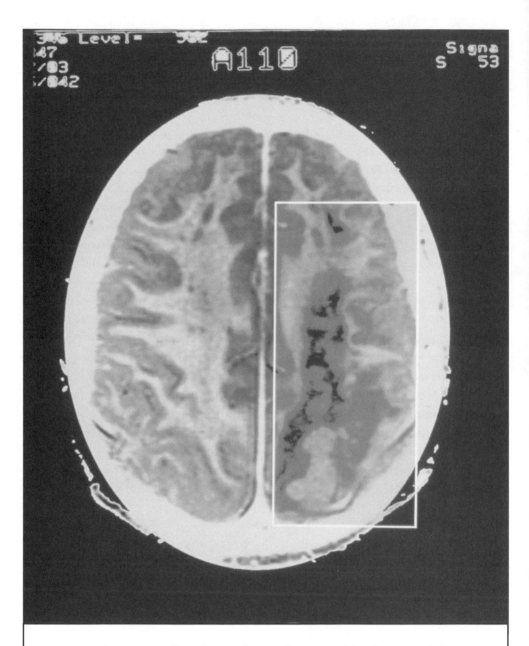

Another cause of stroke is a hemorrhage in a blood vessel of the brain. The dark areas in the boxed area in this view of a brain show blood that has hemorrhaged into the skull.

stroke. In the case of David's grandfather, before he could be given the clot-dissolving medication, a CT scan was performed to make sure that a hemorrhagic stroke was not in progress. If a hemorrhagic stroke were present, a strong blood-thinning drug would have worsened brain bleeding and probably led to death.

New Treatments for Stroke

The use of clot-dissolving agents to treat some forms of stroke represents great progress. Five or ten years ago, David's grandfather would have had permanent damage to the parts of his brain controlling speech and movement and might have lived out his life in a wheelchair or bed.

Today, if strokes are caused by blood clots, remedies include clot-dissolving medications, blood thinning treatments, and drugs such as aspirin that make platelets less sticky. Platelets are a kind of blood cell that helps to form blood clots after a vessel injury. The platelets are shaped like microscopic dishes, and that is the reason for the name. When vessel injury is caused by external trauma, such as a knife wound, platelets get involved. They become sticky and gather together to make a blood clot. This clot fastens to the place of injury and prevents blood loss and death. However, this natural response doesn't help if the blood vessel injury is internal, caused by cholesterol plaque. In this situation, a less sticky platelet is better because a blood clot could be fatal.

Aspirin-like drugs have been used as painkillers since ancient times. In the mid-twentieth century the ability of aspirin to prevent blood clotting was noted. New drugs that make platelets less sticky have been introduced for use in stroke. These drugs, ticlopidine and clopidogrel, act like aspirin without causing stomach irritation, as aspirin often does. Drugs designed to protect and preserve brain tissue in the midst of a stroke are being studied.

For people who have had a stroke, rehabilitation services are essential because they may stimulate neighboring areas of the brain to pick up some of the functions that the damaged control centers can no longer perform. Rehabilitation often includes physical therapy, speech therapy, and occupational therapy.

New forms of surgery are helpful in treating or preventing stroke. In Althea's case, a carotid artery operation prevented another attack by clearing a critical channel of cholesterol deposits. In an approach now being developed, a stent (cylindrical metal framework) is inserted in the carotid artery to keep it open. The stent is inserted through a tiny hole in a leg artery. Under X-ray guidance, the stent is passed to the carotid artery in the neck, then enlarged by inflating a small balloon, and left in the artery. Researchers hope this new method can help to prevent future strokes.

When a hemorrhagic or bleeding stroke occurs, blood thinning is to be avoided. Surgery to relieve pressure in the

Rehabilitation for a person who has had a stroke may include relearning how to walk, speak, and write.

brain and to remove accumulated blood is frequently successful in such cases. When a brain aneurysm, or blood vessel
weakening, is identified, surgery can be performed to remove
it or strengthen the affected area.

Can Stroke Be Prevented?

In the middle of the twentieth century, stroke caused by high
blood pressure was a common cause of death and disability in
the United States. Yet no one thought that lowering blood
pressure could reduce the frequency of stroke. It was thought
that for some people very high blood pressure was necessary to
feed the organs with nourishing blood.

By the 1970s, however, a number of studies showed that
drugs for lowering blood pressure could dramatically reduce
stroke. So stroke could be prevented after all. A public education campaign, still in progress, urges individuals to have their
blood pressure checked and treated. As a result, the incidence
of fatal strokes has decreased over the past twenty years.
Another factor in this improvement is a reduction in tobacco
use. In 1960, 76 percent of adult men in America smoked cig-
arettes. In 1995, only 27 percent did. The percentage of
women and young people who smoke remains high. Studies
are underway to look at the possibility of reducing stroke
through better control of blood sugar (diabetes). Other studies
may demonstrate that regular aerobic exercise, a low-fat diet,
and maintenance of an ideal body weight will also contribute
to stroke prevention.

The question of whether strokes can be prevented by drugs
that lower blood cholesterol is now being explored. The idea
seems to make sense: if cholesterol deposits cause some forms of
stroke, and lowering blood cholesterol stops cholesterol
deposits from forming in vessels, then couldn't stroke be prevented by cholesterol-lowering drugs? In 1994 and 1996, two
large studies seemed to support the idea.[7] Significantly fewer
strokes occurred in heart patients taking cholesterol-lowering
medications compared to an equal group taking placebo (fake)
pills. Simvastatin and pravastatin, the drugs used in the studies,

work to lower cholesterol by slowing down the liver's natural cholesterol-making machinery. In the two studies, strokes were reduced regardless of whether the patient's cholesterol level was high or normal to begin with. New studies are planned to see if cholesterol-lowering treatment can prevent a second stroke.

The use of anti-oxidant vitamins such as vitamin E is being studied in stroke prevention because the chemical reaction in which cholesterol is oxidized seems important to the growth of a cholesterol plaque. Some doctors have proposed the use of estrogen and related new drugs like raloxifene to prevent stroke. These ideas are being studied. In one large project, the WEST study (Women's Estrogen and Stroke Trial), participants are given either estrogen or a placebo and are followed for signs of stroke over several years.

Oxygen Shortage Leads to Vanishing Minds

Simon was playing rugby at his high school reunion when he suffered a major heart attack. A near fatal heart rhythm disturbance followed and Simon stopped breathing. His friends tried to give cardiopulmonary resuscitation (CPR), but no one had any real training in the technique. After ten long minutes, paramedics arrived and gave Simon an electric shock, successfully correcting his heart rhythm right on the field. He survived, but because his brain had been without oxygen for too long, he is impaired. He is conscious, yet speaks only a few words, recognizes no one, and is unable to say who he is, where he is, or what year it is.

Karen was a bright and attractive high school student, but she was insecure socially. At a party some kids talked her into trying heroin. She had never used hard drugs before and was nervous. Someone gave her a glass of vodka to calm her down, and then injected heroin into a vein. When she lost consciousness and stopped breathing, the partygoers panicked and ran. Later Karen was found, alive but in a coma.

Samantha was five years old, riding in a van with her family, when their vehicle skidded on an ice-covered bridge. Witnesses saw the van plunge into the freezing waters and sink. Onlookers

Administering CPR to a person who has had a heart attack

stood helpless, waiting for help to arrive. Nearly one hour later, when rescue workers and police divers pulled them out of the water, Samantha and the other passengers were cold and lifeless. All the victims were transferred by helicopter to a major hospital where they were placed on breathing machines. Samantha's body temperature was 80 degrees Fahrenheit. She and the others had warm fluids poured into all body cavities and her blood was circulated through a warming device. After her body temperature rose to 98 degrees and the water was cleared from her lungs, Samantha awoke. She was the only one to survive.

Martha sat in her car in the middle of winter, waiting for her daughter Antonia at the bus stop. Because the bus was late and the temperature below zero, Martha started the engine so she could use the heater. She became drowsy and dropped off

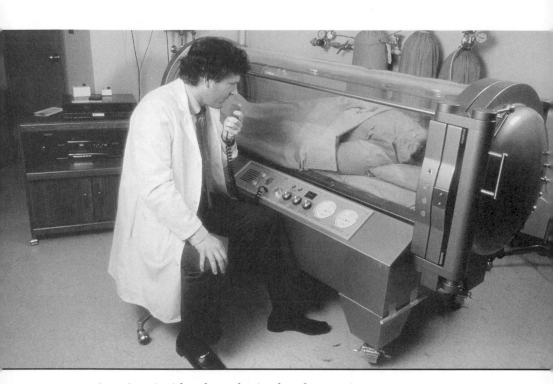

A patient inside a hyperbaric chamber receives pure oxygen under high pressure.

to sleep. When the bus arrived ninety minutes later, Antonia could not rouse her mother. At the hospital Martha's blood tests showed high levels of carbon monoxide, a colorless, odorless gas that had leaked into the car's interior because of a faulty exhaust system. The carbon monoxide had displaced nearly all of the oxygen in her bloodstream, so doctors gave her high doses of oxygen and placed her in a hyperbaric (high-pressure) chamber. Here, pure oxygen was pumped into the sealed area under pressure many times that of the atmosphere at sea level. In this way, the maximum amount of oxygen would be forced into Martha's bloodstream so her brain and vital organs could recover from carbon monoxide poisoning.

Simon, Karen, Samantha, and Martha all suffered brain damage (anoxic brain injury) from lack of oxygen. When oxygen deprivation is total and permanent, death results. The brain centers that govern breathing have been starved of oxygen. In many cases, oxygen can be restored in time to save the hardy breathing centers but not the sensitive emotional and intellectual parts of the brain that make us human. So the body lives on, but the brain dies.

Of the four people described here, Simon, Karen, and Martha are alive but severely impaired. Only the young child, Samantha, made a full recovery. It is not uncommon for cold-water drowning victims who are young to survive and recover. It may be that the preserving effect of cold temperatures, combined with the excellent blood flow and resiliency of young brain cells, rescues them. But this is simply a theory and has not been proven. The best therapy is prevention of accidents and a thorough knowledge of CPR to prevent serious brain injury by assuring an adequate supply of oxygen to the brain during an emergency.

CHAPTER EIGHT

Brain Death by Toxic Chemicals, Drugs, and Diet

Skip is an old man who lives near the docks, collecting his government checks and spending them in the next few days on lottery tickets. He does not drink much anymore and he seems too confused to eat properly. He gets some meals at the soup kitchen and he sleeps at the homeless shelter. Skip has been examined at the local clinic where he was diagnosed as having chronic brain damage, probably partly due to lack of vitamins. The toxic chemicals from the pesticide plant where he used to work may have also played a part in his dementia. Skip survives with the help of some local shopkeepers and charity, but barely. Huge numbers of his brain cells no longer function.

All human brains are influenced by the array of chemicals to which they are exposed. Only certain substances can pass through the tightly connected cells between the blood and the cerebrospinal fluid that bathes the brain. But toxic chemicals can get into your body and reach your brain by way of your blood when you inhale them through your nose and mouth (carbon monoxide), when they penetrate your skin (pesticides), or when you ingest them (lead).

Mercury

New restrictions and attention to environmental hazards such as lead, manganese, and mercury, do a good job of protecting us generally. But lack of knowledge about these toxins can lead to tragic exposures. Mercury is a shiny metal that fascinates children. Most children and many adults do not know that mercury is toxic, especially to brain tissue. In the cultures of some immigrants from the West Indies and Latin America, mercury is believed to have magical powers, and small amounts are sometimes added to bath water, perfume, or water for washing floors. It is also used in spiritual ceremonies. Children who are exposed to it may be slowly poisoned.[1]

In 1998, two teens vandalized an abandoned factory where mercury had been used in the manufacture of neon lights. They found forty pounds of mercury and had great fun dipping their hands and arms in the shiny liquid metal. Through the teens, the mercury was spread to school lockers, homes, and people as far away as fifteen miles in what became a full toxic emergency. A family dog died, some homes had to be evacuated, and many people became sick and may have suffered brain damage.[2]

When Lewis Carroll wrote *Alice in Wonderland*, his readers were probably well aware of the reason for the Mad Hatter's mental problems. In those days, mercury was used in the processing of felt for hats, and hatters were frequently affected by it. Mercury that is part of a compound such as mercury chloride is especially toxic. The importance of keeping these compounds from polluting the seas became evident in a major tragedy in Japan in the 1950s. Until then, mercury compounds were dumped into Japanese waters as waste, and mercury was absorbed by aquatic plants. Fish in those waters fed on the contaminated plants, and then people ate the fish. These people developed many serious problems, especially with their vision. The illness was named the Minimata disease for the town in which many of the affected people lived. In 1999 Minimata disease was observed in populations along the Tapajos River in Brazil, where mercury is used by gold miners.[3]

Lead

The effect of lead on the human body is well known. When it is absorbed, it can cause permanent brain damage and significantly

Information programs are now helping to reduce instances of
lead poisoning among children. A photo from the 1950s shows
a two-year-old about to leave the hospital four months after
brain surgery to relieve the pressure cause by lead deposits. He
had chewed on wood coated with lead-containing paint.

affect a person's intelligence. One out of eleven American preschool-age children is believed to have elevated levels of lead in his or her body due to exposure to the lead-based paint that was used in many houses built before 1980, and to the lead that leaches into drinking water from lead pipes. Federal agencies and other groups are still trying to prevent and cope with lead poisoning.[4] The dark writing compound contained in pencils, though called lead, is actually ordinary graphite, a harmless form of carbon.

Aluminum

Some other metals are suspected of destroying neurons and promoting dementia, too. One of these is aluminum. Some years ago, aluminum was suspected of being a cause of Alzheimer's disease, and many people threw away their aluminum cooking utensils. It has since been shown that aluminum from foil and from pots and pans does not get into food. Even the aluminum that occurs naturally in potatoes and some other foods is not absorbed well by the body. Although a number of subsequent studies have been unable to confirm earlier hypotheses that aluminum is involved in Alzheimer's, there is still some uncertainty about whether aluminum might play a part.[5]

Zinc and Copper

Zinc has been implicated in Alzheimer's disease too, but research has yielded confusing results. Copper may play a role in the degeneration of brain tissue found in Creutzfeldt-Jakob disease in humans and in mad cow disease in cattle.[6] Much remains to be learned about the possibility of brain damage by these and other kinds of chemical poisoning.

Street Drugs

Many street drugs contribute to brain death. Tinkering with the chemistry of the brain by using mind-altering drugs is very dangerous and can cause a variety of problems, including serious allergic reactions, overdose, and death.

Drug deaths often make headlines, especially when rock stars or other celebrities die. The list of those who have overdosed on heroin includes many famous performers and athletes. Despite the headlines that give evidence of the risks, drug abuse remains a significant problem among rock stars. Industry leaders work to convince performers and the public that drug use doesn't enhance talent. All drugs do, they point out, is kill the rockers.[7]

Despite educational campaigns and headlines revealing that another addict has been found dead in a motel room along with syringes and other drug paraphernalia, drugs continue to seduce young people. But chemicals that cause highs also change the chemistry of the brain. Some kinds of drugs act on areas of the brain that regulate respiration, causing breathing to slow nearly to the point of nonexistence. Some drugs interfere with the electrical activity in the brain, and others cause tremors, dizziness, nausea, and rapid heartbeat.

A dramatic example of how drugs affect the brain occurred in 1982. A bad batch of synthetic heroin led to a mysterious paralysis. The underground chemist who produced this drug had accidentally used a chemical that attacked and destroyed a small region in the brain. This was the same part of the brain that is destroyed in Parkinson's disease and the users of the drug found themselves even more severely affected than many who suffer from the disease. They were "frozen" in place, unable to move their arms and legs. Dr. J. William Langston, a neurologist, "unfroze" the addicts with levodopa, one of the drugs used to treat Parkinson's.

Many drug users suffer from the effects of impurities, as well as from the drugs themselves. In some cases, first-time users have an exaggerated reaction to cocaine and they die.[8] In many others, a bad trip means a visit to the emergency room.

Brain damage is common among young people who use inhalants. Paint thinner—a mixture of toluene, acetone, and methanol—is readily available, and its fumes may be sniffed by kids. Various cements and adhesives, dry cleaning fluids,

Glue-sniffing kids can end up with brain damage.

paints, and a long list of other volatile substances have a high potential for abuse as inhalants. Sniffing, huffing, bagging, and spraying are common ways of inhaling vapors to get a high. All of the methods can cause brain damage and lead to death.

When Brian inhaled a waterproofing spray he went into a coma. His friends called 911 and he was rushed to the emergency room of the nearby clinic. Doctors said that he had starved his brain of oxygen because chemicals in the spray temporarily replaced the oxygen. He recovered after three months, but many users damage their brains to the point of death.

A cocaine overdose can be caused by a very small amount of the drug. Sometimes the first use of cocaine or crack (smokable cocaine) can kill. There have been cases of seizures and heart attacks after a first use, even when the person appeared healthy before use. There is no way to predict who will die from cocaine and who will not. Death may come in a variety of ways, one of them being a brain hemorrhage. PCP (phencyclidine)—which is commonly known as angel dust, love boat, killer weed, peace pill, and other names—is another street drug that can cause a toxic reaction and death. There are many others.

Suppose you saw someone suffering from an overdose. His skin looks gray-green, and his eyes roll back in his head. His breathing is shallow. Would you know what to do? A person who is suffering from a drug overdose needs help at once. The best way to prevent a severely drugged brain from seriously depressing a person's breathing is to keep the person awake and get him or her to a hospital emergency room by calling 911. Artificial respiration should be used only if the breathing has stopped, and it may be necessary until medical help is available.

Alcohol
Alcohol is the most commonly abused drug and one that can damage the brain in a number of ways when used excessively. Long-term use of alcohol can cause damage to the frontal lobes of the brain and overall reduction in brain size. Excessive drinking of alcohol is listed as a possible risk factor for Alzheimer's disease and it is certain that it can permanently affect a person's thinking and memory.[9] It also damages the cerebellum, the region of the brain that controls coordination.

The ability to absorb vitamin B1 (thiamine) is impaired in the digestive system of alcoholics, and this, along with poor nutrition, may cause the development of Wernicke's encephalopathy. A person afflicted with this disease suffers confusion, impaired memory, and lack of coordination.

Fred, a heavy drinker for ten years, suffers from the most serious effect of lack of vitamin B1 due to alcohol abuse, a disease called Korsakoff's syndrome. He can remember things that happened a dozen years ago, and his overall intelligence remains intact. But Fred cannot remember current events for more than a few seconds. He finds it impossible to solve problems and, since he cannot remember new things, he cannot absorb new information. In some cases, sufferers of Korsakoff's syndrome forget long periods of their lives, extending as far back as twenty years. Or they may give convincing, detailed accounts of events that never happened. Fortunately, Korsakoff's syndrome is uncommon.

Blackouts after heavy drinking are much more common. In movies, people sometimes cannot remember whether or not they committed a crime when they were drunk the night before. This is true in real life, too. Many drinkers report difficulty in remembering what happened when they were drinking heavily.

Lisa was awake all through the party on Saturday night and she seemed to be thinking reasonably well. Sunday morning,

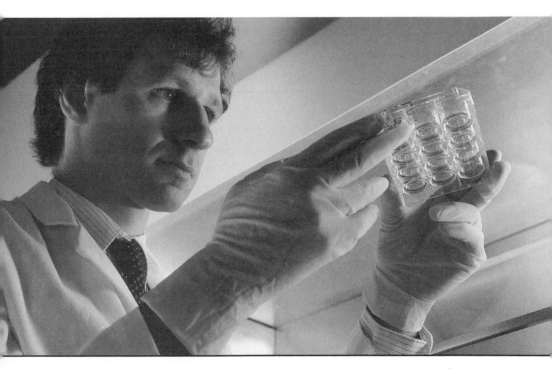

Researchers are actively investigating the genetic component of alcoholism.

she could not remember a conversation she had had with a friend who was at the party, or anything else about what had happened there. Although she did not actually black out, she suffered from a temporary amnesia. Since alcohol acts somewhat like an anesthetic in blunting emotional responses, Lisa's brain did not retain what was taking place. Her memories were "blacked out" because they were never locked into her brain in the first place. People who suffer from blackouts generally have a serious drinking problem.

Binge drinking, the consumption of five or more drinks in a row, is a concern on many campuses. Alcohol is a depressant, and enough of it can decrease breathing and cause a coma and even death. Every year, the deaths of college students from alcohol poisoning are highly publicized. These and many other alcohol-related deaths bring attention to the fact that consumption of alcohol can be deadly.

Diet

Since alcoholics often have poor diets, it is not surprising that they are high on the list of people who suffer brain damage from lack of necessary vitamins. Nutrition scientists have long known that severe deficiencies in B vitamins may adversely affect brain cells.[10] For example, niacin (vitamin B3) is one of the vitamins essential to the normal functioning of the brain and nervous system. A severe deficiency of niacin and some other nutrients causes pellagra, a disease with many symptoms, including nervous system effects: tremors, anxiety, confusion, dementia, irritability, and depression. Niacin deficiency was originally seen in cultures with diets that relied on corn prepared in a way that left niacin in a nonabsorbable state.[11] People with difficulties absorbing food—alcoholics, the elderly who neglect their diets, some infants and pregnant women—are among those at risk of niacin deficiency. Chicken, fish, wheat bran, peanuts, beef, and whole grain wheat products are all rich sources of niacin. This vitamin is found in other foods, too, so it is unlikely that anyone eating a reasonably sound diet will be deficient.

90

Vegetarians are usually a healthy group but need to be careful to add vitamin B12 to their diets. Vitamin B12 is found in significant amounts only in animal-protein foods. Although it is not produced by animals and plants, it is present in bacteria that work their way into animal milk, muscles, and some organs. Only minute amounts of B12 are required.

So meat-eating humans get plenty of vitamin B12. Vegetarians can get enough vitamin B12 through supplements (the chemical name is cyanocobalamin). Vitamin B12 is known as the "energy vitamin," and it is essential for the health of the nervous system. One of the first symptoms of deficiency of this vitamin may be mood changes and mental slowness.[12]

B12 deficiency can lead to permanent damage of the nervous system, including spinal cord and brain degeneration, and a specific type of anemia called pernicious anemia. Fatigue and anemia may be symptoms that call for a check of the blood level of B12.

Dementia may also be associated with dietary deficiencies of other B vitamins, tryptophan, zinc, selenium, calcium, and vitamins C, D, and E.[13] Other chemicals and drugs, as well as diseases such as hypothyroidism, may be responsible for killing neurons to the point of muddled thinking and worse.

While it is not possible to avoid all of the things toxic to human brain cells, knowledge of specific dangers can help you to recognize a problem. Early diagnosis can often cure the problem or prevent further trouble.

CHAPTER NINE

Life-and-Death Choices
When the Brain Dies First

Who should make the life-and-death decisions when the brain dies first? The case of Karen Ann Quinlan called attention to the plight of people who live on after the thinking parts of their brains have died. Twenty-one-year-old Karen Ann Quinlan collapsed on April 15, 1975, possibly as the result of taking a painkiller, Darvon, before drinking a number of gin and tonics at a restaurant. She soon entered a deep coma from which she never recovered. Although her parents believed that she would not want to continue to live in this "persistent vegetative state," she was kept alive through the use of life support systems. A respirator helped her breathe through a hole cut into her throat. Intravenous fluids and antibiotics were pumped into her body. But she showed signs of severe brain damage.

After three months, the Quinlans, with the support of their parish priest, requested that doctors disconnect the respirator because there was no hope of her recovery. The doctors and hospital administrators refused the request because of concern about whether removing the respirator was morally or medically justified. The Quinlans, who wanted peace for their daughter, took the case to court. After a year, the courts allowed medical treatment to be stopped, but Quinlan was still to be tube-fed. By this time, her body had wound itself into a three-foot-long fetal ball, and she continued as a living corpse, weighing only sixty-nine pounds when she finally died of pneumonia in June 1985.[1]

The Quinlan family was at the center of a debate over the right to die after their daughter, Karen Ann Quinlan, was left in a deep coma.

In addition to calling attention to the tragedy of bodies that live after brains have died, the Quinlan case was important for another reason. It clarified the need for guardians to have the right to make treatment decisions based on what patients had requested before they became unable to act for themselves. New laws were passed protecting people from unwanted medical treatment, at least in some cases. Since then, many people have signed "living wills" in which they specify the conditions in which they do not wish to be kept alive. A living will indicates that one wants certain treatments withheld or withdrawn if they only prolong the dying process or if there is no hope of recovery.

The case of Nancy Cruzan, who was injured when she lost control of her car in 1983 and whose brain died before her body, also influenced the movement to prepare advance health-care directives, such as living wills, health proxies, and powers of attorney in which a person is authorized to make decisions for someone unable to do so. After the accident, Nancy Cruzan did not have the ability to swallow and was fed though a tube. She was paralyzed and oblivious to her surroundings, with no chance of recovery. Her brain had degenerated.

When Nancy Cruzan's parents requested that she be allowed to die, the request was refused. This resulted in a debate that reached the U.S. Supreme Court. In 1990, the Court ruled that the refusal of medical treatment must have been expressed by the patient when she was still competent, and that Cruzan had not made her treatment wishes clear in advance. The court said that her parents had not offered "clear and convincing evidence" that she would have wanted to die. This was the first judicial decision dealing with advance directives, and one that led to the formation of many groups that support and encourage the drafting of living wills.

Nancy Cruzan's parents later produced evidence of her wishes, and federal and Missouri courts allowed them to request the removal of their daughter's feeding tube. The inscription on her tombstone reads:

NANCY BETH CRUZAN
MOST BELOVED
DAUGHTER SISTER AUNT

BORN July 20, 1957
DEPARTED Jan. 11, 1983
AT PEACE Dec. 26, 1990[2]

The Right-to-Die Debate Today

While the achievements of modern medicine prolong and enhance life for many patients, some are kept alive after they no longer have any hope of leading meaningful lives or recovering. A dying, elderly man contemplates in terror the possibility that he might be kept on life-support systems. Friends share the agonizing, slow death of a young man with AIDS. A son visits his mother each week in a nursing home where she begs to die before Alzheimer's disease destroys more of her brain.

End-of-life decisions have become the subject of public debate. It is not uncommon to find people at parties, at workshops, and in their doctors' offices expressing opinions about what is right and wrong about euthanasia (bringing about an easy death for a person with incurable disease) and assisted suicide. Opinions vary widely. Many people approve of a quiet, merciful death for a terminally ill patient. Some condone the much publicized actions of Dr. Jack Kevorkian, who has assisted about 130 terminally ill people to take their own lives.[3] In some of these cases, death took place in a makeshift bed in a van when the patient pushed a plunger that allowed a deadly drug to enter his or her bloodstream. The patient was unconscious in twenty-five seconds and the drug stopped the heart and brought death within six minutes.

In September 1998, Dr. Kevorkian gave Thomas Youk, who was suffering from Lou Gerhig's disease, a lethal injection of drugs and recorded his death on videotape. This time Dr.

95

Kevorkian was tried and convicted of second degree murder and sentenced to serve a prison term.

Thousands of people have joined the Hemlock Society, a group that supports the option of suicide for the terminally ill, seeks to educate the public about the rights of the dying, and makes available practical information for ending life. Other right-to-die groups oppose these so-called suicide manuals. They fear that the manuals may be misused by depressed people who are not terminally ill.[4]

Groups such as Compassion in Dying, Choice in Dying, Dying Well Network, and Death with Dignity, encourage education and action to ensure a humane death. Some people feel that the assisted-suicide debate has been fueled by fears about the quality of care for dying patients. Doctors in many hospitals are providing pain management along with attention to emotional and spiritual matters, reaching far beyond the standard realm of medicine.[5] Now that people are more conscious of the dying process, they show more concern about the quality of life at the end.[6]

Surveys have shown that doctors throughout the United States have privately helped their terminally ill patients die. In 1997, Oregon became the first state to permit physician-assisted suicide in limited circumstances. That same year, the U.S. Supreme Court held that state bans on physician-assisted suicide do not violate the U.S. Constitution. The decision of whether to ban it is left up to the individual states. The decision to allow physician-assisted suicide applies only to those of sound mind who have been given less that six months to live.

The debate about the right to die continues among religious, ethical, and medical groups and many complicated issues are involved. One issue is deciding what is right for a patient who is brain dead. Making one's wishes known in the form of a living will is an important step for the young as well as the old.

Most states allow family members to make decisions for their loved ones whose brains have died, even without prior documentation. Some states, however, require clear and convincing evidence that the patient, if competent, would have chosen to die. A "health care power of attorney" allows you to name someone to make health decisions for you if you cannot.

Fifteen-year-old Sara has spent the last five years in a nursing home, where she has excellent care. Her parents lovingly feed her every meal, which has been ground into mush so that she can swallow it. But Sara is oblivious to everything around her. When her mother passes her hand in front of Sara's face, she does not blink. This family feels that Sara should be kept alive until she dies a natural death. Other people who knew Sara feel that she would not want to live this way. Her thinking brain has died, but her brain stem continues to keep her breathing. What will happen to Sara if her family can no longer care for her? Might feeding her ground-up food be considered keeping her alive by extraordinary means?

Dr. C. Everett Koop, former U.S. Surgeon General, states that the Hippocratic oath does not require that the act of dying ever be prolonged. "If my patient has received all that I can do for him, and healing is not possible, I can alleviate his suffering and still stay well within the bounds of 'do no harm.'"[7]

Rosalynn Carter, former first lady, author of *Helping Yourself Help Others*, and honorary chair of the Last Acts Coalition, is quoted as saying, "People's greatest fears revolve around how they will live with illness until they die."[8] The Last Acts Coalition, which includes seventy-two prominent organizations, seeks to change our culture so that death is not seen as a failure, but as a natural process. They seek reforms that will lead to fewer people dying alone, in pain, attached to machines. They believe that more people should experience dying as the last act in the journey of life. Last Acts encourage medical professionals to recognize when and how to stop treatment of dying patients. For those who are partially brain dead, a living will may determine the length of their dying process.

CHAPTER TEN

Caring for Millions of Dying Brains

"Losing a Million Minds: Confronting the Tragedy of Alzheimer's Disease and Other Dementias" is the title of a booklet published by the U.S. Office of Technology Assessment in 1987. A decade later, this might have been titled "Losing Five Million Minds." In 1997, about 4 million people suffered from Alzheimer's disease and many more had other kinds of dementia. Although most of today's young people can look forward to robust health as they grow old, a staggering number of the aging will develop disorders of the brain.

Even when today's teens reach middle age, diseases of the brain will be disproportionately important. What will this mean to you? The population of the United States is now over 276 million and is expected to pass 400 million shortly after the year 2050. The oldest of the old, people over eighty, are now the fastest growing group of the population. One of the known risk factors for Alzheimer's disease is age.[1] Estimates of the number of people who have Alzheimer's by the age of eighty-five are as high as 50 percent.[2] Who will care for all these people? While nursing homes, home care, and assisted living units suffice in many areas of the country today, will there be a place for everyone in the future?

The Cost of Dementia
Disorders of the brain are a varied and costly group of ailments. According to a study sponsored by the National Foundation for

Brain Research, the impact of brain and central nervous system disorders on the United States economy topped $400 billion in 1992.[3] This total includes the cost of hospital care plus an allowance for lost wages and productivity due to neurological disorders, psychiatric diseases, the effects of alcohol, and other drug abuse. Unless better ways are discovered to treat, prevent, or postpone these diseases, the costs to the nation will grow exponentially in the years to come.[4] In addition to the cost in dollars, there is no way to measure the increased emotional cost.

Where Can People Go to Die?

About 80 percent of people in the United States die in hospitals or nursing homes, where, in many cases, modern medicine prolongs the dying process.[5] Jan does not seem concerned about what will happen to her parents when they are old, even if they suffer from dementia. She says they can go to a hospice. Today, hospice care gives emotional, spiritual, physical and medical support to about 14 percent of dying Americans.[6] Usually the care is offered at home, but a limited number of people live at hospice centers. Jan may not realize that not everyone is eligible for hospice care. Patients accepted by a hospice are judged to be within six months of dying. They must acknowledge that they are dying and give up any medical treatment except pain relief. The number of people with dementia who fit hospice requirements is limited. Those who stay in their own homes must have full-time caregivers.

The United States is awash in scholarly studies of the care of the elderly and the dying, ranging from pain management and hospice care to assisted suicide. Health care providers are striving to improve the care of the dying, but many people are unaware of the need for change.

Caring for a Grandparent

Today many people ask "What support is available for my grandmother with vascular dementia?" "How can we deal with a grandfather with Alzheimer's?" Caring for someone whose brain dies first can require major changes in a family's life. Emily and her parents are an example of this phenomenon.

Emily is a eighteen-year-old who has a busy life with school, soccer, swimming, and friends. Her older sister and brother are away at college, and she has been the center of attention in her family for the last two years. Her father coaches the girl's soccer team, and her mother, who works part time, entertains the team after each game.

When Emily's grandfather came to live with them, things changed. Her mother stopped making spaghetti dinners and spent most of her free time caring for her father, who was then in the early stages of Alzheimer's disease. He put things in strange places, forgot what he was saying, and was no longer the man Emily had loved. As her grandfather grew worse, her mother told Emily that she would need her help. Emily was sometimes asked to drive him to the doctor, or stay with him at home. She felt that he could still take care of himself but her parents saw that he really was not aware enough to handle unexpected situations. Emily sometimes resented having to "baby-sit," then felt guilty about it.

In time, things got worse. Her grandfather could no longer dress himself; he was difficult and needed help bathing and using the bathroom. Sometimes he did not recognize anyone; on other days, he seemed like his old self. It was hard to watch him grow more confused as his brain slowly died. It was hard for Emily's mother to give up her own interests and neglect the other members of her family. She called the local chapter of the Alzheimer's Association to find out about respite care—short-term help to give caregivers a break or time to tend to other matters. Respite care might send someone to help with housework, or allow her a weekend away with her husband, or offer understanding and companionship. Through the association, she hired a woman to take care of her father one day a week, but this was expensive. Neither Medicare nor his insurance policy covered the care of a person with dementia. Emily's family knew that there would be heavy expenses for a nursing home in the future, so they tried to save by limiting respite care.

Adult day care was another way for Emily's mother to have some time away from her father's problems. The nearest day treatment program for the elderly was twenty-five miles away and transportation was not available, so Emily drove her grandfather to the center two days a week before she went to school. Her father brought him home at the end of the day.

Emily loved her grandfather, but his disease made life difficult for the family. Emily's mother was exhausted, and after four years, the fami-

Adult day care facilities are one resource for families of an Alzheimer's patient.

ly decided it was necessary to place him in a nursing home. Choosing one was difficult. Some were too expensive; some seemed to neglect patients; others had waiting lists. Finally, they found one an hour's ride away.

A nursing home was the only answer the family could find. Once her grandfather's finances were exhausted, Medicaid, the federal health care program for the poor, would pay for his care until he died. When he was near the end of his life, the family tried to be with him as much as possible. But Emily felt that he had died a long time earlier.

Home Care

In addition to the 4 million people who now suffer from Alzheimer's, 3 to 4 million caregivers are affected. Taking care of someone with Alzheimer's or other kinds of dementia extracts a tremendous toll in stress, health risks, and lost educational and career opportunities. Many people cannot afford home help, and some cannot find nursing homes. Studies show that nearly one in four American families is taking care of a sick elderly relative or friend.[7] African-Americans are twice as likely as whites to receive their primary care from family members when their health declines.[8]

When Ted was fifty years old, his mother, Nina, who lived alone in New Jersey, had a stroke. In addition to paralysis of her right side, her brain suffered considerable damage. Her doctor called Ted who was living in California and made it clear that his mother could no longer care for herself. Ted brought his mother to California so that he and other nearby family members could care for her. He felt responsible for the care of his aging parent. For those who have no one, a nursing home may become their new home. For some, the street is home until they die.

Scattered and fractured families that are already straining to raise children find caring for elderly parents near the end of their lives extremely difficult. This is especially true when the brain dies first and the illness is long.

Knowing When It Is Time to Die

Helen lived with her daughter, Margarita, for five years after her Alzheimer's disease was first recognized. When Helen developed pneumonia, her doctor suggested an expensive antibiotic to keep her alive. Another doctor suggested that the family let the pneumonia take its course. Margarita felt she should do everything possible to help her mother, so she agreed to the medication. Her mother recovered from the pneumonia but remained in a coma. She never spoke again or understood anything that was said to her. Margarita wondered if she should have listened to the doctor who suggested they stop aggressive treatment. In the difficult years that followed, Margarita sometimes felt that her mother had really died before she had even developed pneumonia.

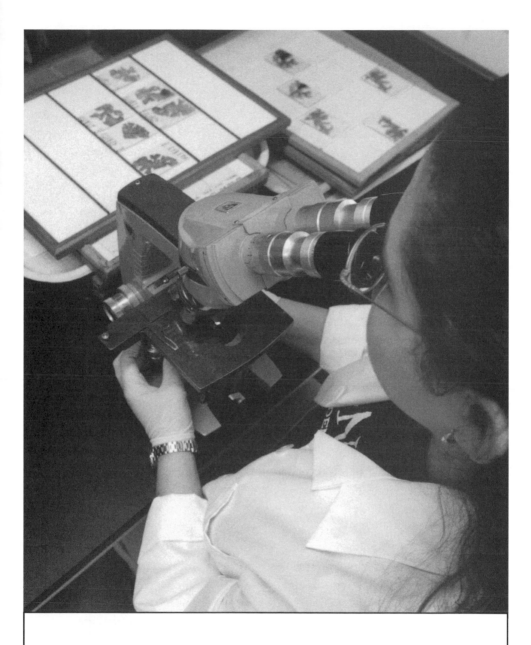

Researchers are working to identify risk factors and causes of Alzheimer's and other forms of dementia.

Brain Death

"When does life end?" is a frequent topic of discussion today. Brain death was defined in 1983 by the President's Commission for the Study of Problems in Medicine as whole-brain death. This means the entire brain—the upper portion that controls consciousness (the cerebral cortex), and the lower brain (the brain stem) that controls breathing and heartbeat.

Cardiac dead used to be as dead as you could be. In the past, you were considered dead if your heart stopped pumping blood. Today, medical technology can keep you alive for years by taking over the functions of your heart and lungs. The current definition of death is brain dead, a condition in which there is no electrical activity in the brain. Still, there is some disagreement about what brain death means. It could mean no activity in the thinking part of the brain, or it could mean no activity in any part of the brain, including the brain stem, which controls many of life's basic function.

An increasing number of people are making their wishes known about end-of-life care. They make it clear that they do not want aggressive treatment when their mental functions have deteriorated. They plan a good death, with the cooperation of their families and doctors.

When Caregiving Is Overwhelming

Imagine the plight of an eighty-two-year-old man who is left in his wheelchair at a park. You see him on your morning run, and he is still there when you walk home later in the day. He seems confused and can't tell you his name. He has no identification, so you call 911. Medics take him away, and you wonder what will happen to him. You wonder how anyone could abandon a helpless old man.

The next day you see a short article in your local paper about the man in the wheelchair. He was left there by his wife, Marcia, and the article tells her story. Marcia had been a loving caregiver for years, but she grew exhausted from the burden of dressing, bathing, and feeding her husband. He needed attention hour after hour, but he only recognized her for a minute now and then. Marcia described her husband as a 150-pound infant who needed constant attention, asked the same questions again and again, and stared blankly at her when he was awake. She could no longer cope with day-to-day living. One morning, in desperation, she took him to the park and left him there. The newspaper said she "dumped" him.

Sometimes victims of Alzheimer's disease and other kinds of dementia are abandoned outside nursing homes, at hospital emergency entrances, and in other public places.[9] In most cases, their caregivers felt the need to run away from their responsibilities. Many of them have cared for a spouse or parent to the point that they have no more money for medicines, hygiene supplies, or even food. Some caregivers are so desperate that they have killed their loved ones and, in some cases, themselves, too.

Help is available for those who can no longer cope with caring for someone who suffers from dementia, and for those who no longer have caregivers. The Eldercare Locater is a nationwide directory service designed to help old persons and their caregivers locate local support resources. It is a public service of the Administration on Aging, of the U.S. Department of Health and Human Services. Anyone can call for information Monday through Friday between the hours of 9 A.M. and 8 P.M. at 800-677-1116.

Of the 4 million Americans with Alzheimer's disease, 70 percent are cared for at home.[10] In most cases, caregivers share the burden with other family members and friends and use programs in their community. The Alzheimer's Association, with more than 200 chapters nationwide, provides information about how to get help, and makes help available to caregivers. This is one of the many places that provides help for people with brain disorders. Other sources of information are listed at the end of this book.

CHAPTER ELEVEN

Keeping the Brain Alive and Healthy

Books about how to improve your brain power, your memory, and your aging mind appear frequently on library shelves. Though these books may suggest ways to become older and wiser and live to be a hundred, much about the health of the brain remains unknown. Thousands of scientists all over the world are searching for ways to unravel the mysteries of brain disorders. Their global attack has yielded new tests, treatments, and cures for many disorders; but for others, medical science has little to offer.

The Congress of the United States designated the ten years beginning January 1, 1990 as the Decade of the Brain to enhance public awareness of the benefits derived from brain research. Thousands of scientists and health care professionals produced numerous studies of the workings of healthy and diseased brains. Since the beginning of the decade, the pace of research on the brain has moved so rapidly that many of its mysteries are being unraveled.

In March of each year, the need for research on all kinds of brain disorders is highlighted by Brain Awareness Week. This is an annual educational campaign sponsored by the Society for Neuroscience and the Dana Alliance for Brain Initiatives, along with over three hundred science, advocacy, and health organizations. Brain Awareness Week demonstrates the importance of research for the health and well being of the American public. You can learn about activities in your area and how to participate in this annual program by contacting the Society for Neuroscience directly or through its web page. See pages 136 and 138.

Which Disease Is This?

The ability to predict the onset of a disease or recognize it in its early stages is particularly important in the case of the brain, for brain damage is often devastating and irreparable.[1] If an illness is misdiagnosed, possible cures may be missed. Tumors, strokes, severe depression, thyroid problems, Alzheimer's, side effects of medications, nutritional disorders, and certain infectious diseases can all have similar effects.[2] But some of these conditions are curable, especially in the early stages.

Can a disease be predicted by genetic testing? Genes are the basic units of heredity that direct almost every aspect of the construction, operation, and repair of living organisms. Genetic research continues to turn up evidence of a link between genes and diseases.

Since research has established that the presence of the gene apolipoprotein E4 (apoE4) may increase the risk of developing Alzheimer's disease, why not test everyone for this gene? A blood test can determine which people have one or a pair of apoE4 genes, but its presence does not predict Alzheimer's with certainty. A person carrying apoE4 may not get the disease, and a person who does not carry it may.[3] Recent research suggests that some other genes may also be involved in increasing the risk of late onset cases.[4]

Although some hereditary factor appears to play a part in the development of Alzheimer's disease, studies indicate that the likelihood that a close relative of an afflicted individual will develop the disease is low. In most cases, such an individual's risk is only slightly higher than that of the general population.[5]

Glutaric aciduria is a hereditary disease that damages a part of the brain. The disease is seen in the Amish community in Lancaster County, Pennsylvania. In many countries, including Germany, Ireland, Sweden, Israel, Saudi Arabia, Canada, and the United States, there are clusters of children with glutaric

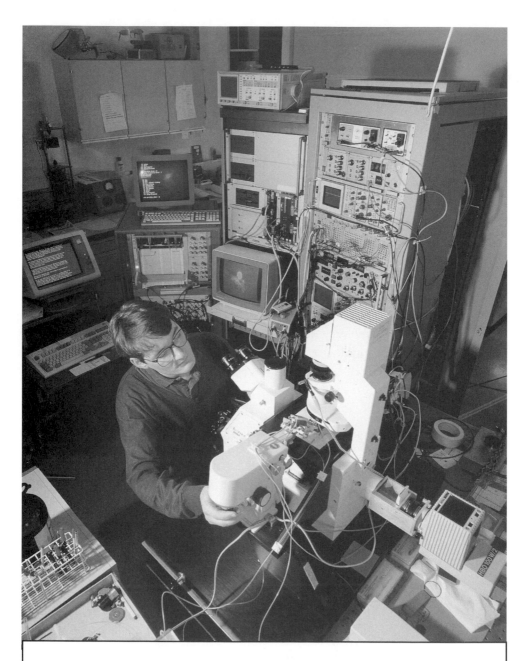

Improved microscopes and other fine instruments allow researchers to probe deeper into the human brain.

aciduria. When these children's bodies are stressed by diseases such as chicken pox or strep throat, they cannot break down certain amino acids in their food normally. The resulting buildup of an abnormal chemical attacks the nervous system and damages the part of the brain that controls bodily movements.

A child with glutaric acidura who is not treated becomes disabled for life and can die at a very young age. Dr. Holmes Morton worked among the Amish beginning in 1987 to learn more about the disease and found that it is hereditary, can be diagnosed during the first few days of life, and can be treated through a special diet. If a child survives the first five years of life, he or she becomes resistant to the worst aspects of the disease.[6]

Why Test?

The perfect tests for predicting many kinds of dementia may be far in the future. Even if there were such a test, would you want to know if you were at risk? A test to detect early stages of a disease would help patients and their families to plan and investigate all possible treatments. So the efforts to develop tests for brain disorders continue.

Prevention

The brain dies before the body for many different reasons. In the case of Alzheimer's, the most common form of dementia, researchers believe that there are many different factors involved and these may vary for each individual. Some of these factors have been mentioned in earlier chapters. Exercising body and brain have long been recommended as prevention against aging, and recent studies have reinforced the importance of such exercise in the prevention of some brain disorders.

Obviously, violence prevention would decrease the damage caused by bullets in the brain and blows to the skull. Avoidance of toxic chemicals, control of infectious diseases, and healthy lifestyles are some of the ways to keep the brain functioning well.

Recently, one study yielded the first strong evidence that intellectual stimulation can significantly increase the number of brain cells in a crucial region of the brains of mice. Until now, researchers believed that an enriched environment enhanced intellectual performance because it increased the number of connections between brain cells. Most scientists assumed that the number of active brain cells was more or less set early in childhood. Now they wonder if environmental factors play a role in recovery from brain injury.[7]

Avoiding head injuries now appears to be important for new reasons, including a possible relationship between these types of injuries and the development of Alzheimer's disease. Although avoidance is not always possible, there are many ways to increase your protection against head injuries. Think First, the National Brain and Spinal Cord Injury Prevention Program, is an award-winning public education effort that targets teens and young adults. Young people are at high risk for devastating injuries from motor vehicle crashes, falls, sports (especially diving and boxing), and violence and can profit from injury-prevention programs such as Think First.

Think First programs operate in forty-seven states. The national office offers free training to start a program, publishes a quarterly newsletter called

Get ready for

Brain Awareness Week

March 15-21

It's a chance for your community to learn about the exciting advances that have been made in brain research!

Brought to you by **The Dana Alliance for Brain Initiatives**. Committed to advancing education about the personal and public benefits of brain research.
www.dana.org/brainweek

Public education programs include "Brain Awareness Week," an annual effort to inform the public about progress in brain research.

Prevention Pages, and has films available for high schools, service clubs, and others concerned about injury prevention. If you are interested in starting a group in your school, contact the Think First Foundation (see page 136).

Causes of Brain Disorders

As mentioned earlier in this book, we now have some of the information needed to explain the mystery of vanishing minds. And brain disorders are being targeted on many fronts with new approaches and new techniques. In the summer of 1997, scientists announced a major medical advance: the discovery of the cause of brain-cell death in certain diseases, including Huntington's. They found that in each case, an insoluble ball of protein forms in the cell nucleus and kills it. They identified genes in Huntington's and in some related diseases that play a part in the development of long strings of excess DNA (the sequences that make up genes). This excess DNA collects into the balls that clog the cells. Until this discovery, the cause of cell death in Huntington's had not been known. By finding this puzzle piece, scientists moved a step closer to learning how to dissolve the balls of protein and how to perhaps someday delay or prevent the onset of the disease.[8]

Researchers who explore the brains of a variety of lower animals help to unravel the mystery of many brain disorders. Mice that have been bred with certain genes are being studied to learn more about the plaques that build up in human brains and interfere with learning and memory.

Clearly, there are multiple forces at work in determining whether a person develops a disease in which the brain dies first. Many of the factors involved in the formation of brain tumors and brain death by infection, toxic chemicals, and other causes remain a mystery.

Searching for Cures

Undiscovered chemicals in the brain may someday be used as medicines to stimulate growth of nerve cells in patients with Parkinson's and Alzheimer's diseases.

Cures may come from a variety of areas. For example, genetic research can reveal the sources and biochemical pathways of disease and lead to the development of safer, more precise, and more powerful treatments. It has already yielded new and more effective medicines to treat stroke.[9]

Brain transplants have long been a part of science fiction, but researchers in the real world are making some use of tissues from embryos for grafts in the brains of adults with Parkinson's disease. Although most research using embryonic cells is centered on illnesses such as Parkinson's disease, Huntington's disease, and juvenile diabetes, scientists are beginning to explore the idea of brain implants for Alzheimer's disease as well. Since the death of neurons is widespread in AD, the use of surgical implants could be more difficult than in conditions where the damage is confined to a smaller area.[10]

A search for new drugs is a major part of the effort to find ways to keep brains healthy and mend those that are not functioning well. The search begins with chemists who study known chemical molecules and develop new ones. Then biologists test the promising molecules in living cells taken from various animal and human organs to discover if they are beneficial. Molecules that pass this test are studied to see if they are toxic to living things. Many drugs never get beyond this stage, either because they are unsafe or because they do not work.

The 1998 announcement of the discovery of the substance called spherons caused great excitement. Spherons appear in everyone's brain tissue by the age of one year and increase in size, becoming a thousand times bigger by the time a person is seventy-five. Many of these big spherons burst. According to researchers at Nymox Pharmaceutical Corporation, where they were discovered, the bursting spherons then become the senile amyloid plaques of Alzheimer's disease. A drug capable of blocking the transformation of spherons into plaques could offer hope for slowing or stopping Alzheimer's disease. However, this theory must be extensively tested before drug research can begin.[11]

Some patients with degenerative diseases hoped that drugs based on spherons would be available a few months after their discovery was announced, but these people were unaware of the long process of drug development and animal testing that must proceed before a new medication is made available. When a pharmaceutical company announces the discovery of a new brain entity, such as spherons, it submits a research application to the Food and Drug Administration (FDA). If the company's plans do not seem too risky, clinical trials are begun to assess which treatments may be most effective for humans.

Paul's wife saw a television announcement calling for volunteers for clinical trials of drugs for degenerative diseases. Knowing that Paul had symptoms of early Alzheimer's, she helped him to volunteer. The application process was extensive and included both physical and mental testing, and Paul's wife had to agree to help as his caregiver and to monitor his drug taking and his progress.

Paul was one of one hundred volunteers who took part in the yearlong Phase 1 of a clinical trial. Neither he nor the staff monitoring the trial knew whether he was receiving the actual drug or a harmless, inert pill—a placebo. Paul and others in the trial were watched closely for possible improvement in their conditions, and were repeatedly tested to see how well the drug was being absorbed, used by the human body, and excreted. If the drug appeared to be safe and effective, Phase 2 would begin.

Typically, between one hundred and three hundred patients take part in the controlled studies of a second phase of a clinical trial. If the drug demonstrates effectiveness in fighting the disease and appears safe, it will move to Phase 3 after a period ranging from several months to two years. In Phase 3, between one thousand and three thousand patients in hospitals, doctors' offices, and clinics take part in the trial, which attempts to confirm the results of the previous phase. If a drug still appears to be safe and effective in this phase, over a period of one to four years, the Food and Drug Administration reviews and evaluates the data. If the FDA approves the drug, doctors may begin prescribing it for their patients.[12]

Many drugs are being explored in efforts to find a substance that will help to keep the brain alive. Scientists are at work at pharmaceutical companies and at government and other research laboratories. The U.S. government's National Institute on Aging and other branches of the National Institutes of Health fund and conduct extensive basic research on brain functioning and disease processes.

One approach in developing medicines for degenerative brain diseases is increasing the brain's supply of acetylcholine, a neurotransmitter that aids communication between neurons in the brain and that is in low supply in brains of people with Alzheimer's. Two medicines that enhance or mimic the supply of acetylcholine have been approved by the FDA; others are in the late stages of the drug-approval process.

Other approaches target drugs that can help delay the death of brain cells. For example, scientists are studying whether the hormone estrogen may work as an antioxidant, stopping the harmful action of oxygen that can damage cells. Other antioxidants—vitamin C, vitamin E, B-carotene, and a number of other vitamins and minerals—may be of value too.

Many doctors think brain inflammation is one step in the development of Alzheimer's, and some studies indicate that anti-inflammatory drugs (NSAIDS or nonsteroidal anti-inflammatory drugs) may lower the risk of degenerative disease. NSAIDS include ibuprofen, indocin, and naproxen. Studies have shown that people who take these drugs over a long period of time for arthritis or rheumatism may be somewhat less likely to develop AD.[13] However, extended use of NSAIDS may cause gastrointestinal bleeding.

Finding a way to help drugs reach the brain is a major problem in the treatment of Alzheimer's, brain tumors, and other brain disorders. The blood-brain barrier, which protects the brain with a tight wall of capillaries and the special cells wrapped around them, provides one obstacle. In addition, certain enzymes act as gatekeepers, escorting only particular substances into the brain.

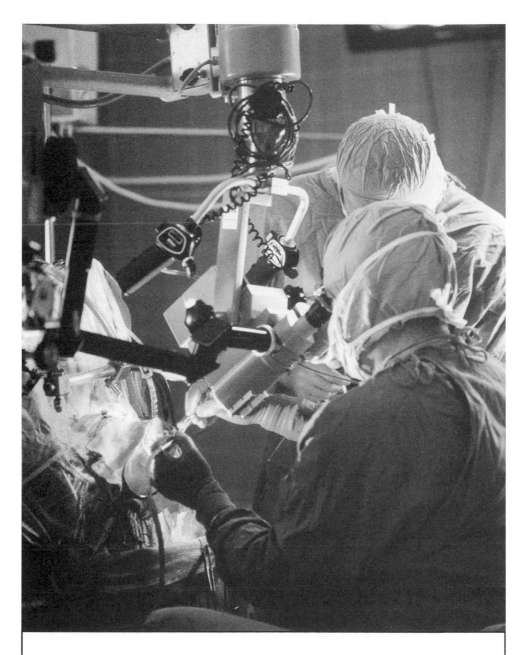

Major advances are occuring in surgery. Here surgeons perform open brain microsurgery.

News of a possible vaccine to fight brain changes tied to AD appeared in July, 1999. When tested in mice, the new vaccine appears to prevent the plaque deposits common in people with AD and to decrease the concentration of plaques where they have formed. Since these experiments are in early stages, it may be years before humans can benefit from such a vaccine. If further tests prove successful, the vaccine might be used to prevent or treat the disease.

The search for new drugs is difficult and expensive, but it is an important approach to finding ways to keep the brain healthy.

Gene Therapy

Many new technologies offer hope for learning more about the brain. One of the most exciting fields of medicine in the last decade has been gene therapy. Scientists first identify the gene that causes a defect, and then try to replace it with the correct version. Genetically engineered viruses may be made to carry normal versions of the faulty gene.

Gene therapy involves some major challenges. One is developing a vehicle to carry genes to a sufficient number of cells. Another is coaxing the genes to "turn on," or do what scientists want them to do. Another is making sure they do their job for a long enough period of time. As gene therapy moves closer to reality, researchers hope to begin studies in humans within the next five years.[14] Gene therapy may some-day supply "smart genes" to the brains of Alzheimer's patients. Most ethicists see no problem with using gene therapy to treat patients with dread diseases.

Some people object to "tampering" with nature, while others feel that experiments with inserting new genes into the body's own cells may be the fastest way of conquering degenerative diseases. Although there are large technological obstacles to finding how to insert genes that correct or prevent problems, some scientists believe that twenty years from now gene therapy will have revolutionized medicine.[15]

From Backrooms to Headlines

A few decades ago, a diagnosis of dementia and other brain disorders was often kept a family secret, for it carried a stigma. The demented elderly were sometimes hidden in attics, while their overburdened caregivers suffered in silence, not knowing where to turn for help. Today the climate is changing dramatically. A child with epilepsy no longer needs to hide the illness. Dementia and other brain disorders have emerged from the shadows and are being treated as major public health problems. News about the brain makes headlines, and hopes for cures come with each new theory.

Just a few of the avenues of research for new drugs to prevent and cure brain disorders have been mentioned in this chapter. Many new ideas and theories are emerging, and new techniques in brain imaging and other technologies hold great promise for learning more about brain disorders.

Great strides have been made in the fight against disorders in which the brain dies first. Although progress seems slow to those waiting for cures, important advances are being made toward keeping the brain healthy.

Chapter 1

1. The Dana Alliance for Brain Initiatives, "Your Source Guide to Information on Brain Disease and Disorders." New York: Dana Press, 1996, p.1.
2. Ibid.
3. National Institute on Aging, *Progress Report on Alzheimer's Disease.* 1997, p. 3.
4. "Alzheimer's Cases Will Quadruple in 50 Years." *Johns Hopkins' News*, September 9, 1998.
5. Richard Restak, *Older and Wiser.* New York: Simon and Schuster, 1997, p. 149.
6. Special Report, "Mind and Brain." *Scientific American*, 1994, pp. 2-5.
7. Sherwin P. Nuland, *Wisdom of the Body.* New York: Knopf, 1997, p. 329.
8. Nancy Andreason, *The Broken Brain.* New York: Harper and Row, 1984, p. 85.
9. Sara Stein, *The Body Book.* New York: Workman, 1992, p. 247.
10. Richard Restak, *The Brain.* New York: Bantam Books, 1979, p. 251.
11. Ibid., p. 246.
12. Miriam Aronson, *Understanding Alzheimer's Disease.* New York: Scribner's, 1988, p. 24.
13. Nuland, pp. 345-346.
14. Steven Pinker, "Can a Computer Be Conscious?" *U.S. News and World Report*, August 18-25, pp. 63-64.
15. Steven Pinker, *How the Mind Works.* New York: Norton, 1997, p. 85.
16. Pinker, "Can a Computer Be Conscious?" pp. 63-64.
17. Ibid.
18. Nuland, p. 329.
19. Anthony Smith, *The Mind.* New York: Viking Press, 1984, p. 96.

20. Donald Stein and others, *Brain Repair*. New York: Oxford University Press, 1995, foreword.

Chapter 2

1. New York Hospital, Aitkin Neuroscience Center, 1997, http://aitkin.org/research.html
2. *American Medical Association Family Medical Guide.* "Cerebral Palsy." New York: Random House, 1994, pp. 716-717.
3. Jacy Showers, "Campaign against Shaking Babies." Groveport, Oh.: *SBS Prevention Plus,* pamphlet, 1994.
4. Nathan Aaseng and Jay Aaseng, *Head Injuries.* New York: FranklinWatts, 1996, p. 36.
5. Ibid.
6. Carey Goldberg, "Pediatric Experts Express Doubt on Au Pair's Defense." *New York Times*, November 12, 1997.
7. American Humane Association, "Shaken Baby Syndrome." Englewood, Colo.: leaflet, p. 2.
8. Jacy Showers, "Shaken Baby Syndrome, Most Commonly Asked Questions." Groveport, Oh.: *SBS Prevention Plus,* pamphlet, 1997.
9. Frank T. Vertosick, *When the Air Hits Your Brain.* New York: Norton, 1996, p. 98.
10. *Medical Tribune News Service,* "Experts Meet to Fight Shaken Baby Syndrome." November 12, 1996.
11. Gina Kolata, "Research Hints at a Gene Link to Brain Afflictions of Boxers." *New York Times*, July 9, 1997.
12. Aaseng and Aaseng, *Head Injuries.* pp. 31-32.
13. Ibid., p. 37.
14. Ibid., p. 36.
15. Ibid., pp. 52-53.

Chapter 3

1. Pamphlet, Aitkin Neuroscience Center. New York: Cornell Medical Center, 1997.

2. William Calvin and George A. Ojemann, *Conversations with Neil's Brain*. Reading. Mass.: Addison-Wesley, 1994, p. 29.

3. David Noonan, *Neuro: Life on the Frontlines of Brain Surgery and Neurological Medicine*. New York: Simon and Schuster, 1989, p. 62.

4. Frank Vertosick, *When Air Hits the Brain*. New York: Ballantine Books, 1996, pp. 233-234.

5. Noonan, p. 63.

6. Ibid., pp. 63-64.

7. http://www.ninds.nih.gov/HEALTHINFO/DISOR DER/BRTUMORS/braintumor.HTM, p. 9.

8. Ibid., p. 3.

9. Robert Youngson, *The Surgery Book*. New York: St. Martins Press, 1993, p. 82.

10. "Removing Half of Brain Improves Young Epileptics' Lives." *New York Times,* August 19, 1997.

11. Ben Carson with Cecil Murphy, *Gifted Hands*. Grand Rapids: Zondervan Books, 1990, pp. 145-162.

12. Ibid., pp. 153-154.

13. Joel L. Swerdlow, "Quiet Miracles of the Brain." *National Geographic,* June 1995, p. 6.

14. "Research Shows Removal of Half a Brain Improves Epileptic's Quality of Life." *Doctor's Guide to Medical and Other News*. Baltimore: PSL Consulting Group, 1997.

Chapter 4

1. Anne M. Haywood, "Transmissible Spongiform Encephalopathies." *New England Journal of Medicine,* December 18, 1997, p. 1821.

2. Ibid.

3. Richard Rhodes, *Deadly Feasts: Tracking the Secrets of a Terrifying New Plague*. New York: Simon and Schuster, 1997, p. 228.

4. *Nutrition News.* Health, January/February 1998, p. 29.
5. Ellen Rupopel Shell, "Could Mad Cow Disease Happen Here?" *Atlantic Monthly.* September 1998, pp. 98, 100.
6. Rhodes, p. 34.
7. Ibid., p. 54.
8. Ibid., p. 50.
9. Ibid., p. 106.
10. Ibid., p. 132.
11. Stanley B. Pruisner, "The Prion Diseases." *Scientific American*, January 1995, http://www.sciam.com0195issues/0195prusiner.html
12. Rhodes, pp. 174-175.
13. Ibid., p. 185.
14. Ibid., p. 223.
15. "W.H.O. Seeks Barriers Against Cow Disease." *New York Times*, April 4, 1996.
16. Rhodes, p. 229.
17. Haywood, p. 1825.
18. "Fear of Disease Prompts Ban on European Imports." *New York Times*, December 14, 1997.
19. "Alarmed by Meningitis, Rhode Island Tried Mass Inoculation." *New York Times*, March 8, 1998.
20. AIDS Dementia Complex Conference. Lemuel Shattuck Hospital, Jamaica Plain, Mass., October 16, 1996.
21. Sherwin B. Nuland, *How We Die*: *Reflections on Life's Final Chapter.* New York: Alfred Knopf, 1994, p. 187.

Chapter 5

1. Caroline McNeil, *Alzheimer's Disease: Unraveling the Mystery.* NIH and NIA, Annual Report 1995, p. 4.
2. Stanley Birge, "The Role of Estrogen in the Treatment and Prevention of Dementia." *American Journal of Medicine*, September 22, 1997, introduction.
3. Paul A. Kettl, "Alzheimer's Disease: An Update." *Hospital Medicine*, October 1997, p. 17.

4. Bruce S. McEwen and Harold M. Schmeck, Jr., *The Hostage Brain*, New York: Rockefeller University Press, 1994, p. 245.
5. *Harvard Health Letter.* May 1997, p. 1.
6. Ibid., p. 2.
7. McNeil, p. 16.
8. "Scientists Find Enzyme Linked to Alzheimer's." *New York Times,* October 22, 1999, p. 1.
9. Dharma Singh Khalsa, *Brain Longevity.* New York: Time Warner Books, 1997, pp. 165-66.
10. McNeil, p. 16.
11. Caroline McNeil, *Progress Report on Alzheimer's Disease 1996.* National Institute on Aging, National Institutes of Health publication no. 96-4137, p. 14.

Chapter 6

1. *Science News*, September 30, 1995, p. 223.
2. *New England Journal of Medicine*, January 29, 1998, p. 278.
3. *Time,* November 23, 1963. http://www.yi.com/home/HelfertManfred/Guthrie.html.
4. George Huntington, "On Chorea." *Medical Surgical Reporter*, v. 26, 1910, p. 317.
5. "Cause of Brain Cells' Death in 7 Diseases Is Discovered," *New York Times*, August 8, 1997.
6. The Parkinson's Web, http://www.parkinson.org/pdedu.htm
7. "Parkinson's Disease." National Institute of Neurological Disorders and Stroke, Pub. 94-139, 1994.
8. Charles Salter, Jr., "Ejner's Hope," *John Hopkins Magazine*, February 1997, pp. 34-40.
9. "Parkinson's Disease," *Mayo Clinic Health Letter*, February 1996, pp. 4-5.
10. Salter, p. 38.
11. Salter, p. 37.
12. Ibid.

13. *Harvard Health Letter.* September 1996, pp. 4-5.
14. Ole Isacson, "On the Brain." *Harvard Mahoney Neuroscience Institute Letter*, 1994, pp. 2-3; http://neuro-surgery.mgh.harvard.edu/oisacson.html

Chapter 7

1. National Stroke Association, http://www.stroke.org
2. Ibid.
3. Ibid.
4. L. Kilander, M.D., Eighth European Meeting on Hypertension. Milan, Italy, June 1997.
5. K. Yaffe and others, "Estrogen Therapy in Postmenopausal Women: Effects on Cognitive Function and Dementia." *Journal of the American Medical Association*, vol. 279, 1998, p. 688.
6. M. Gunel, R. P. Lifton, "News and Views: Counting Strokes." *Nature Genetics,* vol. 13, 1996, p. 384.
7. Scandanavian Simvastatin Survival Study Group, "Randomized Trial of Cholesterol Lowering in 4444 Patients with Coronary Heart Disease." *Lancet,* vol. 344, 1994, p. 1383; F. Sacks and others, "Cholesterol and Recurrent Events." *New England Journal of Medicine,* vol. 335, 1996, p. 1001.

Chapter 8

1. Mirta Ojito, "Ritual Use of Mercury Prompts Testing of Children for Poisoning." *New York Times,* December 14, 1997.
2. "The Quicksilver Mess." *Time,* January 26, 1998.
3. http://www.amazonia.net/Articles/155.htm
4. Irene Kessel and John O'Connor, *Getting the Lead Out: The Complete Resource on How to Prevent and Cope with Lead Poisoning.* New York: Plenum Press, 1997.
5. Carolyn McNeil, *Alzheimer's Disease: Unraveling the Mystery.* Bethesda, Md.: National Institute on Aging, 1995, pp. 20, 22.

6. "News Flash, Copper and Mad Cow Disease Linked?" http://www.alzheimers.com/site/NEWS
7. Michael Goldberg, "Editorial Rant." www.addict.com/-issues/1.11/Up_Front/Editorial_Rant/p. 2.
8. Daryl S. Inaba, *Uppers, Downers, and All Arounders.* Ashland, Ore.: CNS Publications, 1997.
9. Elaine Landau, *Alzheimer's Disease.* New York: Franklin Watts, 1996, p. 48.
10. "Smarten Up." *Tufts University Health and Nutrition Letter*, February 1998, pp. 4-5.
11. "Niacin," www.ozemail.com.au/~bookman/niacin.html
12. Elson M. Haas, "Staying Healthy with Nutrition." quoted in http://www.healthy.net/library/books/haas/vitamins/b12.html
13. "Dementia." http://www.moreton.com.au/ana/hand book/dem.html, p. 2.

Chapter 9

1. Marilyn Webb, *The Good Death.* New York: Bantam Books, 1997, pp. 131-52.
2. Howard Spiro and others, *Facing Death.* New Haven, Conn.: Yale University Press, 1996, p. 100.
3. "Kevorkian Deaths Total 100." *New York Times*, March 15, 1998.
4. George Howe Colt, *The Enigma of Suicide.* New York: Simon and Schuster, 1991, p. 373.
5. "The Cries of the Dying Awaken Doctors to a New Approach, Palliative Care." *New York Times*, June 30, 1997.
6. Lawrence O. Gostin, "Deciding Life and Death in the Courtroom." *Journal of the American Medical Association,* November 12, 1997, p. 1523.
7. Joni Eareckson Tada, *When Is It Right to Die?* Grand Rapids, Mich.: Zondervan, 1992, p. 184.

8. "New Coalition Launched to Improve Care of Dying; Rosalynn Carter Will Be Honorary Chair of 'Last Acts,'" http:www.lastacts.org/roscart/html, Washington, D.C.: Last Acts, 1997.

Chapter 10

1. Caroline McNeil, *Progress Report on Alzheimer's Disease 1996.* Silver Spring, Md.: National Institute on Aging, p. 21.
2. Ibid., 1997, p. 6.
3. www.the-scientist.library.upenn.edu/yrl1996/sept/kreeger_pl_960916.html
4. *Preparing for the Senior Boom.* Ad Hoc Group for Medical Research Funding, NIH, Bethesda, Md., 1998, p. 1.
5. John Horgan, "Seeking a Better Way to Die." *Scientific American,* May 1997, p. 100.
6. "At the End of Life, a Blind Bureaucracy." *New York Times,* March 11, 1998.
7. Ibid.
8. "Blacks Carry Load of Care for Their Elderly," *New York Times,* March 15, 1998.
9. Ibid.
10. "Caregiver Stress: Signs to Watch For...Steps to Take." Leaflet. Chicago, Ill.: Alzheimer's Association, 1998. p. 1.

Chapter 11

1. Bruce S. McEwen and Harold M. Schmeck, Jr. *The Hostage Brain.* New York: Rockefeller University Press, 1994, p. 256.
2. Carolyn McNeil, *Progress Report on Alzheimer's Disease, 1998.* Silver Spring, Md.: National Institute on Aging, p. 26.
3. McNeil, p. 12.
4. http://www.alzheimers.org/pub/genefact.html
5. U.S. Dept. of Health and Human Services, www.health gate.com/HealthGate/hic/alz/b.index.html, 1997.

6. "Heroes of Medicine." *Time*, special issue, Fall 1997, pp. 31-32.
7. Donald G. Stein and others, *Brain Repair.* New York: Oxford University Press, 1994, VIII, pp. 73.
8. "Cause of Brain Cells' Death in 7 Diseases Is Discovered." *New York Times*, August 8, 1997.
9. http://www.phrma.org/issues/genetic.html
10. Elaine Landau, *Alzheimer's Disease.* New York: Franklin Watts, 1996, pp. 77-76.
11. http://www.nymox.com/press.htm, March 16, 1998.
12. Ibid.
13. Neil Cutler and John Srameck, *Understanding Alzheimer's Disease.* Jackson: University Press of Mississippi, 1996.
14. Sean Henahan, "Gene Therapy for Alzheimer's?" http://www.gene.com/ae/WN/SU/alz496.html
15. "Keys to the Kingdom," *Time*, special issue, Fall 1996, pp. 24-29.

Acetylcholine: a neurotransmitter found in reduced levels in people with Alzheimer's disease.

Axon: a single fiber that carries nerve impulses away from the cell body. Each nerve cell has a single axon that may be as long as one foot.

Blood-brain barrier: a network of membranes between the circulating blood and the brain. The blood-brain barrier allows only certain substances through and is the brain's first line of defense against harmful substances.

Brain stem: the core of structures between the spinal cord and the cerebral hemispheres of the brain, including the medulla, pons, and midbrain.

Brain tumor: an abnormal growth in the brain caused by cells reproducing in an uncontrolled manner.

Cerebrospinal fluid: a clear, watery substance found in the skull and spinal cord. It cushions the brain and maintains a constant rate of pressure.

Cerebrum: the largest and uppermost portion of the brain.

Clinical trials: carefully controlled studies to test the value of drugs, surgery, or other treatments for disease in humans.

Computerized tomography (CT or CAT) scan: a device that takes a series of X-ray images which are compiled by a computer into two-dimensional "slices" showing a highly detailed picture.

Cortex: outermost layer of cells of the cerebrum; "bark" of the cerebrum.

Dementia: a group of symptoms that characterizes certain diseases and conditions. Loss of intellectual abilities, such as memory capacity, severe enough to interfere with social or occupational functioning.

Dendrite: one of the fine filaments that branch off from the body of a nerve cell. The receiver of messages.

Dopamine: a neurotransmitter.

Free radicals: see "oxygen free radicals."

Glial cell: a type of brain cell that provides nourishment and support for the neurons.

Hemispherectomy: an operation in which a large portion of the brain is removed to alleviate uncontrollable seizures.

Hippocampus: a large curved structure in the brain believed to play a part in memory.

Living will: a document that describes preferences for medical steps to be taken if the person becomes unable to make decisions.

Metabolism: the normal bodily process of turning food into energy.

Nerve growth factor: a chemical produced by the body that promotes the health of acetylcholine-producing cells.

Neuritic plaque: an abnormal cluster of protein, dead and dying nerve cells, and other cells. One of the characteristic features found in the brain during autopsy of a person who had Alzheimer's disease.

Neurofibrillary tangle: an accumulation of twisted protein fragments inside nerve cells, whose presence helps to determine Alzheimer's disease upon autopsy.

Neuron: the structural unit of the nervous system; a nerve cell.

Neurosurgery: the science and art of operating on the nervous system.

Neurotransmitter: a chemical messenger released by a neuron to act on another neuron at a synapse.

Oxygen free radicals: oxygen molecules with unpaired electrons that are highly reactive; which combine readily with other molecules and sometimes cause damage to cells.

Pallidotomy: a surgical procedure that destroys a small amount of tissue deep within the brain to relieve some of the symptoms of Parkinson's disease.

Paranoia: a term used to describe a person who falsely believes that he or she is being persecuted.

Plaques and tangles: see "neuritic plaque" and "neurofibrillary tangle."

Power of attorney: a legal document giving another person authority to make financial and legal decisions if the principal becomes physically or mentally incompetent.

Prion: a particle of protein believed to be involved in spongiform diseases.

Serotonin: a neurotransmitter.

Spheron: a protein that may be the forerunner of senile plaques in the aged human brain of Alzheimer's patients.

Synapse: the space between neurons through which they communicate.

Ventricles: fluid-filled cavities within the brain.

Books

Aaseng, Nathan and Jay Aaseng. *Head Injuries*. New York: Franklin Watts, 1996.

Barmeier, Jim. *The Brain*. San Diego: Lucent, 1996.

Benson, Herbert. *Timeless Healing*. New York: Scribner, 1996.

Calvin, William H., and George A. Ojeman. *Conversations with Neil's Brain: The Neural Nature of Thought and Language*. Reading, Mass.: Addison Wesley, 1994.

Hyde, Margaret O. *Mind Drugs*, 6th ed. Brookfield, Conn.: Millbrook, 1998.

Landau, Elaine. *Alzheimer's Disease*. New York: Franklin Watts, 1996.

McEwen, Bruce S., and Harold M. Schmeck, Jr. *The Hostage Brain*. New York: Rockefeller University Press, 1994.

Noonan, David. *Neuro: Life on the Frontlines of Brain Surgery and Neurological Medicine*. New York: Simon and Schuster, 1989.

Nuland, Sherwin B. *How We Die: Reflections on Life's Final Chapter*. New York: Simon and Schuster, 1989.

Rhodes, Richard. *Deadly Feasts: Tracking the Secrets of a Terrifying New Plague*. New York: Simon and Schuster, 1997.

Stein, Donald, Simon Brailowsky, and Bruno Will. *Brain Repair*. New York: Oxford University Press, 1995.

Vertosick, Frank T. *When the Air Hits Your Brain: Tales of Neurosurgery*. New York: W. W. Norton, 1996.

Organizations

Alzheimer's Association
National Office
919 N. Michigan Avenue, Suite 1000
Chicago, IL 60611
800-272-3900

Alzheimer's Disease Education and Referral Center (ADEAR Center)
P.O. Box 8250
Silver Spring, MD 20907-8250
800-438-4380

American Association of Suicidology
4201 Connecticut Avenue, NW, Suite 310
Washington, DC 20008
202-237-2280

American Brain Tumor Association
2720 River Road, Suite 146
Des Plaines, IL 60018
800-886-2282

American Parkinson's Disease Association
1250 Hylan Blvd.
Staten Island, NY 10305
800-223-2732

Batten's Disease Support and Research Association
2600 Parsons Avenue
Columbus, OH 43207
800-448-4570

Brain Trauma Foundation
555 Madison Avenue, Suite 200
New York, NY 10022-3303
212-753-5003

The Brain Tumor Society
84 Seattle Street
Boston, MA 02134-1245
800-770-8287 (TBTS)

CDC National AIDS Clearinghouse
P.O. Box 6003
Rockville, MD 20849-6003
800-458-5231
800-342-AIDS (English)
800-344-SIDA (Spanish)
800-243-7889 (TTY)

Children's Brain Disease Foundation
350 Parnassus Avenue, Suite 900
San Francisco, CA 94117
415-565-6259

The Children's Brain Tumor Foundation
247 Madison Avenue, Suite 1301
New York, NY 10016
212-448-9494

The Dana Alliance for Brain Initiatives
745 Fifth Avenue, Suite 700
New York, NY 10151
212-223-4040

The Epilepsy Foundation of America
4351 Garden City Drive
Landover, MD 20785
800-332-1000

Family Caregiver Alliance
425 Bush Street, Suite 500
San Francisco, CA 94108
415-434-3388

Hereditary Disease Foundation
1427 Seventh Street, Suite 2
Santa Monica, CA 90401
310-458-4183

Huntington's Disease Society of America
140 W. 22nd Street, 6th Floor
New York, NY 10011-2420
212-242-1968 (24-hour message)
800-345-4372

Hydrocephalus Association
870 Market Street, Suite 955
San Francisco, CA 94102
415-732-7040

Multiple Sclerosis Association of America
706 Haddenfield Road
Cherry Hill, NJ 08022
800-LEARN MS

National Brain Tumor Foundation
785 Market Street, Suite 1600
San Francisco, CA 94103
800-934-CURE

National Foundation for Brain Research
 1250 24th St., NW, Suite 300
Washington, DC 20037
202-293-5453

National Head Injury Foundation
1776 Massachusetts Avenue, NW, #100
Washington, DC 20036
800-444-6443

National Institutes of Health
Neurological Institute
P.O. Box 5801
Bethesda, MD 20824
800-352-9424

National Institute of Neurological Disorders and Stroke
Building 31, Room 8A-16
31 Center Drive
MSC 2540
Bethesda, MD 20892-2540
800-352-9424

National Institute of Neurological Disorders and Stroke
The Office of Scientific and Health Reports
9000 Rockville Pike, Rm. 8Al6
Bethesda, MD 20892
800-352-9424

National Institute on Aging
Public Information Office
Bldg. 31, Rm. 5C27
31 Center Drive, MSC2292
Bethesda, MD 20892
800-222-2225

National Neimann-Pick Foundation
22201 Riverpoint Trail
Carrollton, VA 23314
804-357-6774

National Parkinson Foundation, Inc.
1501 NW 9th Avenue, Rm. 4013
Miami, FL 33136
800-327-4545 (National)
800-433-7022 (FL residents)

National Organization for Rare Disorders (NORD)
P.O. Box 8923
New Fairfield, CT 06812-1783
800-999-6673

National Stroke Association
96 Inverness Drive East, Suite 1
Englewood, CO 80112-5112
800-STROKES

Society for Neuroscience
11 Dupont Circle NW #500
Washington, DC 20036
202-462-6688

Think First Foundation
22 S. Washington Street
Park Ridge, IL 60068
800-Think56

Internet Sources

Alzheimer's Association
http://www.alz.org

Alzheimer's Disease Education and Referral Center (ADEAR Center)
http://www.alzheimers.org/adear

American Brain Tumor Association
http://www.abta.org

American Parkinson's Disease Association
http://www.apda.parkinson.com

Batten's Disease Support and Research Association
http://www.bdsra.org

CDC National AIDS Clearinghouse
http://www.cdcnac.org

The Children's Brain Tumor Foundation
http://www.childrensneuronet.org

The Dana Alliance for Brain Initiatives
http://www.dana.org

The Epilepsy Foundation of America
http://www.efa.org

Heredity Disease Foundation
http://www.hdfoundation.org

Huntington's Disease Society of America
http://neuro-www2.mgh.harvard.edu/hdsa/hdsamain.nclk

Hydrocephalus Association
http://www.neurosurgery.mgh.harvard/ha

Multiple Sclerosis Association of America
http://www.msaa.com

National Brain Tumor Foundation
http://www.braintumor.org

National Foundation for Brain Research
http://www.brainnet.org

National Institute of Neurological Disorders and Stroke
http://www.ninds.nih.gov

National Institute on Aging
http://www.nih.gov/nia

National Parkinson Foundation, Inc.
http://www.parkinson.org

National Stroke Association
http://www.stroke.org

Neuroscience for Kids
http://faculty.washington.edu/~chudler/neurok.html

Society for Neuroscience
http://www.sfu.org

Page numbers in *italics* indicate illustrations

and gun violence, 26-28, 39, 109

and head injuries, 6, 7, *7*, 16, 18-28, 51-52, 110

healthy functioning of, 8-15, *9*

and infection, 16, 30, 33, 33-43, 85, 111

and oxygen deprivation, 78-81, 87

parts of, 10, 30-32, 57, 61, 64, 88

pressure in 25-26

and stroke, 50, 54, 64, 66-78, 88, 102, 112

surgery, 26, 27, 28-29, *28, 29,* 30-32, 63-65, *115*

and toxins, 6, 16, 50, 82-85, 109, 111

transplants, 112

tumors, 28-30, 107, 111, 114

viruses, 6, 16, 33, 51, 55, 60

Brain Awareness Week, 106-7

Brain imaging equipment, *20,* 21, 25, 26, 27, *40,* 49, 63, 64, 68, 75, *108*

Brain "pacemaker," 64-64, *65*

Cancer, 29-30, 43

Carbidopa, 62

Carbon monoxide, 80, 82

Cardiopulmonary resuscitation (CPR), 78, *79*

Cardiovascular diseases, 52

Carotid artery, 66, 71, 72

Carotid artery operations, 76

Carotid endarterectomy, 72

Carson, Ben, 30-32

Carter, Rosalynn, 97

Center for Cognitive Science, 13

Central nervous system, 16, 42, 54, 99. *See also* Nervous system

Cerebellum, 88

Cerebral artery, *69*

Cerebral cortex, 10, 104

Cerebral hemorrhage, 73

Cerebral palsy, 16, *17,* 20

Cerebrospinal fluid, 21, 23, 26, 82

Cerebrum, 10

Cervical collars, 24, *25*

Child abuse, 16, 18-21

Choice in Dying, 96

Cholesterol, 68, 71, 72, 75, 76, 77-78

Cholesterol-lowering medications, 77-78

Clopidogrel, 75

Cocaine, 86, 87-87

Comas, 21, 27, 73, 78, 87, 90, 102

Compassion in Dying, 96

Concussions, 52

Convulsions, 18

Copper, 85

Cortical Lewy bodies, 56

Cortisol, 52

Coumadin, 71

Crack cocaine, 86-87

Creutzfeldt-Jakob disease (CJD), 33, *34,* 35, 37-39, 85

Cruzan, Nancy, 94-95

CT (computerized tomography) scans, 25, 26, 27, *40,* 49, 68, 75

Cyanocobalamin, 91